THE E

LIVES OF TWO VERY

ORDINARY PEOPLE

Will Hinton

Published by White Feather Press.
(www.whitefeatherpress.com)

ISBN 978-1-61808-189-6
Printed in the United States of America

White Feather Press

Reaffirming Faith in God, Family and Country

Dedication

First, foremost, and most important, this must be for my Lord and Savior Jesus Christ. Without Him my life would have been really messed up. Let's face it, even with His wonderful love and guidance I still managed to do that in a few places!

Next has to be to Donna, the love of my life for 51 wonderful years. And how could I not remember Dorothy, the great love He sent to love me through the next "however many" years as my dear helpmate. She sustains me so very well.

My two wonderful children, Doug and Beth and their spouses, Kim and Mike. I am so proud and happy with who and what they are.

Then those five fine grandsons of ours; wow, has God ever blessed us through them. Plus, if you would have told me many years ago that I would end up with at least five GREAT grandkids, in addition to the grandsons, I would have laughed at you.

I shudder to imagine what those tiny ones might have to go through in this fallen and falling world in the years to come.

My prayer is for them to rely on the One Who has brought me through to this point in such a glorious and blessed way and that they will have the families like mine to bless and keep them.

Shalom.

Will

Prologue

I had pulled into Toledo Express airport late on a Sunday night, hoping there might be someone at the hanger where I was to start work the following day who could guide me to someplace to rent a room for the night. I found better than that, for a pilot who rented a room from a homeowner by the week had just flown in from a charter. He had me follow him to Swanton, Ohio, and arranged a room for me that was to be my home for a time.

He left me with instructions to meet him at the "restaurant up next to the railroad tracks for breakfast in the morning."

The next morning I was at the counter beside Otis, (his name) when I heard the click-clack of high heels on the tile floor. Being young, single, and normal I looked to see the originator of those sounds. What I saw was this petite little gal in high heels, a full skirt that was fitted at the bodice, and auburn hair.

I watched intently as she made her way to the end of the counter and turned the corner to face our direction and pay the cashier. Her face was so very pretty to go with the rest of the sweet little figure.

As I watched, I received an elbow to the ribs from Otis and he said, "Now son, there's one to take home to mama." I was later to take his advice. But I should really start at the beginning, so let me catch you up to this place in my story. First, a disclaimer: I tell this story only to glorify the One Who directed most of my life; that One is Jesus Christ. I have come to realize He has interacted so often and so clearly in our lives that the story needs telling to glorify Him.

Plus, this is more of my dear wife Donna's story than it is mine, because of the way she glorified Him with her love and devotion. I will boldly proclaim that NO ONE ever loved Jesus MORE than she did and does. Not Peter, not James, not John; nobody.

During the first week after her death, our daughter Beth said to me, "Just think, Dad, Mom might be talking to Grandma or Grandpa right now."

I replied, "I don't think so." Beth looked at me in shock until I said, "She hasn't taken her eyes off of Jesus yet."

With that as the end of my start to my/our story, please allow me to get to the specifics of our starts in life, the extraordinary lives of two very ordinary people. God has been truly amazing!!

Listen my son, to your father's instruction and do not forsake your mother's teaching. They will be a garland to grace your head and a chain to adorn your neck.

Proverbs 1:8&9 (NIV)

Chapter One

MY LIFE STARTED ON FEBRU-
ary fourteenth in 1940. I was born at
home during the worst snowstorm they
had seen for many years. I've been told that my dad and
grandfather had to dig paths through four-foot drifts to get
the doctor to the house. I can't affirm that because I was
too busy to remember! Crying is hard work, you know.

My mother, Hazel Mirinda Davis Hinton, was Clyde
G. Hinton's second wife and I was his fifth child. Dad's
first wife had been tragically killed a year and a half before when she rode horseback into a field with a nasty
bull. The bull charged the horse, goring it and throwing
my siblings' mother into a post of some sort, breaking her
back.

Dad's children before me were my oldest brother, (you
can say half-brother if you want, but we saw ourselves as
a family and never used the term) Clyde Junior, (not the
term for junior, but his actual middle name) Constance,
Carlos, and Charles (Chuck.)

1

Chuck was only six months old at the time; Dad was running a large dairy farm besides being a busy dad, so my grandparents took Chuck to help out. By the time Dad married Mom, who lived on that same farm in a tenement house with her father and brother, his parents had become solidly attached to Chuck and Grandma, and protested loudly when Dad wanted him back. Mom won.

That set the family up for a potential trouble spot years later, but that's a story for a later chapter.

During WWII Dad worked as a welder in Canton, Ohio, building cargo booms for Navy ships. We were moved to a rental house near Waterford, Ohio and Dad hitched rides home for weekends. Once the war was over he went back to farming, this time on a farm near what

The old barn we actually used for the cows and horses. Plus the outhouse, which we also used.

was known as Palmer Square. This was a square mile laid out just like the northwestern corner of Ohio, except it was the only place with enough flat area to accomplish such a feat in Washington County.

Around age fourteen, the start
of a love affair with guitars

Just to demonstrate how far medicine has come, when I was six, Dad had a hernia operation and they told him he had to stay in bed for several weeks, plus, he couldn't farm any more because of the lifting. This always makes me crack up, because Dad decided if he couldn't farm, he would build houses. Wait a minute; is there not heavy lifting while building houses? I still chuckle over that.

3

So, we moved once again, about a quarter of a mile back up a lane to the house on the hill right above where we had been! That became "the home place" and the fond location of the majority of my adventures, or maybe misadventures in some cases, while growing up. It was a 65-acre farm with over 25 acres of woods. Yep, you're right; I lived in those woods.

The huge difference in my formative years came with that move. My Grandpa Davis, a farrier and horse trader, retired from the trade because of arthritis in his shoulders that prevented him from shoeing the larger work horses. He just couldn't handle them any more. The beauty of the thing for me was, that not only did we still have our farm team from the previous place, but "Gramps" brought other horses with him to add to that number. I was in heaven, and I rode most of the daylight hours when I could.

This takes us through the first six, almost seven years of my life, and it is not my intention to chronicle all of my adventures and misadventures while growing up, but rather to show the supreme intervention of God in my life right from the start.

My son, do not forget my teaching, but keep my commandments in your heart, for they will prolong your life many years and bring you prosperity.`

                      Proverbs 3:1-4 (NIV)

Chapter Two

DONNA BANKS WAS BORN A twin on September 8, 1937. She weighed three pounds and Donald weighed nine. Wow, not a good start, but she overcame that and ended up a fine young lady.

Donna was the third daughter of Chester and Helen Banks, and her older siblings were: June, Ardith, then twins Darrell and Dennis, and finally she and Don. I like to tell folks that Donna had THREE twin brothers just to watch the wheels of their minds start whirling faster.

Her dad was a railroader and was gone a lot, but he showed them what a dad's love was about when he was home. Mother was a homemaker of the highest degree. (I always called her Mother out of love as much as out of respect. She was a dear lady.)

Donna shared with me that much of her childhood was spent doing the typical little girl things along with three boisterous brothers to pick on her. Donna remained small in physical stature, reaching 104 pounds on a good day to go with her 5'2" height. She might have been small, but with her almost reticent personality and a true love for others, she shined at life.

When Donna was 15, she was associating with several friends who attended church and youth activities often, and they were instrumental in her becoming a Christian. She used to chuckle when telling me about their church activities, because she did not have much follow up after accepting Christ, and every so often she would go forward to do so again! I would tease her about what a sinner she must have been to need salvation so many times. That was always good for the little pointed elbow in the ribs if she was close enough.

As she studied the Word she became more at ease with her salvation and ended up a spiritual giant. After high school graduation, she worked at a local factory in the office, but after nearly a year she began to feel the call to the mission field. She answered that call in the manner she would use for the rest of her life: with total obedience.

While Donna was getting saved and closer to Christ, the Hintons attended church at Palmer, but no one ever sat me down and explained that I could and should have a personal relationship with Jesus Christ. They were sincere people who taught us, but not very skilled at it. Thus I grew up acknowledging there was a God, and believing that Jesus was real, and God's Son, but no relationship developed.

Extraordinary Lives

Listen my son, accept what I
say and the years of your life
will be many. 13: Hold on to
instruction, do not let it go;
guard it well, for it is your life.

Proverbs 4:10 & 13:10 (NIV)

Chapter Three

SOME PEOPLE MIGHT THINK growing up in a farm home with no running water or indoor plumbing a real handicap and detrimental to maturity; I believe otherwise. In fact, I cherish the legacy I have from my childhood. We heated with wood or coal, took what few baths we took in a galvanized tub with water heated on the wood stove, and used an outhouse located some thirty yards from the house.

My bedroom had no heat whatsoever, and I learned to pull the covers around my face in the winter in a manner that left only my nose and mouth exposed to the atmosphere. I would later endure much teasing for that in Navy boot camp until I broke the habit! Fortunately, no one ever thought of giving me ostrich for a nickname!

Four things controlled my life during, and even after my childhood. I loved to read, and as soon as I could, Mom had me reading the works of Zane Grey, her favorite author. I was around eight when that occurred. Next was my love of animals, and especially horses; I literally lived on a horse much of my formative years. What intelligent, magnificent creatures God has placed here for us!

Next was guitar music, and I would finally buckle down at age 14 to learn to play. There was a time in my life when all I wanted to be known as was a guitar player! And finally, those majestic, fascinating, intoxicating machines that flew over our little farm: airplanes!

My parent's patience must have been that of Job, because during many meals my chair would fly backwards, and the screen door would be banging on the spring several times because I heard an engine far in the distance and tore out to stand frozen, staring and entranced as I watched them travel from horizon to horizon. That love would eventually shape my life to a great extent. While aviation shaped my life and made it a total adventure, the other three loves added much as well. For a backward, shy country boy to experience the life I have is nothing short of storybook material, which is why I am writing this. Thing is, Donna is the one (with God's help) who served to shape me into the person I finally became. But … I'm getting ahead of myself.

I need to share a few of my childhood exploits simply to familiarize you with the personality and outlook I had. (And still retain much of them, I'm afraid.)

We were hunters. Everyone in my family hunted, and we ate what we shot, including groundhogs. Hey, quit your grimacing; they are vegetarians! Properly cooked, they are quite good. We had safety training, although it wasn't officially called that; we were just taken out in the field and taught how to safely use a gun.

Once we demonstrated the proper use as we hunted with the adults, we were then turned loose to hunt alone. The only stipulation was that we always let Mom know when and where on the farm we were going.

I was given my first .22 rifle by Grandpa Davis and told I could hunt alone when I was eight. You read that right, age eight. Never even considered shooting at a hu-

Old Champ and Will, Good buddies.

man being. You see, with all the trouble we're having in this country and world today with shootings; guns are not the problem; PARENTS ARE!

That's right; parents are not raising their children right. Too many parents are either too lazy to do that, or they think they are to be best buddies of their children and so refrain from discipline. I have news for you parents, you can and should discipline your children, and when done right, you WILL be their best friend.

Every Thanksgiving and Christmas time we organized a family hunt. Dad, we three boys, and sister Connie's husband would get in a line and walk the entire farm, as well as a couple of adjoining woods, for rabbits. The yell, "There he goes!" still rings in my ears. The shooter

Will's first pony, old Polly

did the skinning, and we all did the eating. Rabbits are wonderful tasting food. The best thing about those hunts, however, was not the success of the hunt, but just the time together after a common goal.

Here I go again, slipping away from the task at hand and preaching instead. Back to the story.

I was very afraid of getting hurt as a child, but didn't have the sense to recognize just what things might cause the pain. For instance, roller skates and I never became familiar friends because I was afraid of falling. I was always hesitant on them.

However, and this should be embarrassing, when I saw a cowboy in the movies doing tricks on a galloping horse, I just had to do that! He would swing off the horse on one side, hit the ground with his feet and swing clear over the steed's back to repeat the trick on the other side; landing in the saddle. I was enthralled and had to do that; never mind that it might hurt if it was done wrong.

I learned to trick ride without any really bad injuries. There was the first time I tried it when my well-trained trail horse slammed on the brakes as soon as I swung out of the saddle, sending me rolling along sans horse in the grass of the pasture. He then trotted over to me and inspected me with curious eyes that asked why I had been so clumsy!

The thing I see as I look back was if a possible adventure involved being like a cowboy, musician, or pilot, I could be counted on to attempt it with no thoughts of pain or injury. But the initial fear of pain never left until I was much "advanced in age." Somewhere in my late twenties I slipped into the realm of "normalcy." Of course, two years of racing a sports car had wedged itself in there somewhere, but more on that later.

The school I attended for the first eight grades was called Palmer, after the "square" I mentioned, and was a two-room affair with only two teachers. There was the "little" room and the "big" room. That referred to the size of the students, not the size of the room. When I was in fourth grade my musical career started; I sang a humorous thing called "Fuedin,' fussin, and fightin'" at the PTA meeting one month. I grabbed onto the thrill of applause and have never gotten enough of public performances since then!

With hearing the lessons being taught for three years by the time you were in the fourth, and later the eighth grade, the lessons had just naturally soaked in by osmosis. Well, for me, anyway. I was blessed with nearly a photographic memory and school was a breeze for those eight years.

I was in sixth grade when this crazy desire to write began to set in. Having heard all those lessons last year, study time while the teacher was working with the other three grades was truly boring. To alleviate that I started writing stories. I used the comic book characters for my people, mostly Donald Duck and friends, and had a blast doing that.

Keep in mind that we had all heard Mrs. Tucker through the dividing wall for four years and had a built-in fear of her. She was one strict lady. (But she loved us one and all.) I was intently writing one day while she had a different grade doing some research or something, and so all was quiet when I suddenly thought my life was over! I was whipping words out ad nauseam when a shadow fell over my desk! I thought I was gonna die. Mrs. Tucker had caught me!

Her big, rawboned hand came into my rapidly blurring vision and picked up the paper, held it in front of her for quite a while, then placed it gently back on my desk. That same hand then rested on my trembling shoulder and she asked me to come see her at recess. I repeat: I thought I was going to die.

She continued her strolling up and down all the aisles for a while until the time was up for whichever class was doing their exercise and then announced recess. My life was over.

I made my way as slowly as possible to her desk and stood waiting for the world to end. Mrs. Tucker was one of the strictest teachers in the world. She had a paddle she used freely that looked like a canoe paddle. She was close to 5' 9" tall and a very rawboned, strong lady with a shrill, loud voice. All of us had spent four years in the next room listening to her bawl out the classes for one thing or another, and we fairly trembled at her presence.

She looked at me and said in a kind, gentle voice, "That is a very good job of writing, Wilbur. I have a question, and if you say no, that will be fine. I would like for you to read your story to the four classes once it's done, and maybe try to have one to do that with for every grade period for the rest of the year. Remember, a no answer is okay."

HA!! With the relief I felt; how could I say no to her? That started a relationship that I never imagined any child could have with that dear lady, and one I treasure the memory of to this day. During the winter she would challenge all of the students to play checkers against her

"Gramps" Davis, a hero!

during recess time, and many of us did. I could beat her half the time and she loved it! After all, I learned to play checkers from a master; my Grandpa Davis.

Just a little bit about Gramps, as we called him; I spent many evenings in his trailer across the driveway eating cheese and crackers while playing checkers or seven up with cards. His impact on my life was at least as powerful as my dad's. His stories became lodged firmly in my memory. I guess now is as good a time as any to explain where my real imagination came from. My Grandma Davis died when Mom was 15, and Mom was her caregiver for the last two years of Grandma's life.

For the last year they made up a game to occupy Grandma since she could no longer read or do much of anything that required any movement.

She taught Mom this, and Mom taught me. We each made up the names of fictional family members, plus other characters, and we verbally role-played those people through adventures we made up as we went along. The result of those exercises for me was constant story formation going on inside my head during each and every waking moment. There are still times I wish I could just turn my mind off and go into neutral!

****

SCHOOL GOT A LITTLE TOUGHER ONCE WE TRANS-ferred to "the big school" in Waterford and the math classes took on a different light. I loved math and took every course the school had, but had to endure a few grades in the B range as a result. Hey, nobody's perfect!

Since we did not have much guidance in that small high school, my folks and I felt college was simply impossible for us to afford. I researched the military schools, saw the Navy offered the longest and most highly technical schools that would allow me to be near airplanes, and took that route.

Not to make her sound less than interesting, please keep in mind that Donna grew up as far away on the other corner of the state as was possible; so I have only snatches of her school days that she shared with me during our 51 years together. From what she shared, it seems she was a totally normal girl with all the normal girl problems and blessings that any youngster has had. Except for her spiritual life, that is.

Her time was spent with girl friends and the youth group at their church with not a lot, if any, dating going on. Her biggest worries were her weight and the concerns that she might never be considered pretty or attractive. I used to tease her when she would tell me that by asking, "You mean you didn't have mirrors then so you could see that you were and are?" That was usually good for the elbow.

Once graduated and working, she, as stated before, began to feel the call to the mission field and responded in obedience. You already know the results of that. I need to get back to my own story in order to chronicle the path

God took me on to cause our lives to join.

Each summer Chuck would come and stay a few days with us, and I actually had a big brother to play with during that time. After all, Carlos, the next in line, was seven years older than me. The reality was that I was basically an only child. Not complaining, just stating a fact, and you'll see why in a bit.

Take a twelve year old "only child" and insert a fourteen year old from another household to begin to take much of the attention, toys, and so on away and you have a recipe for disaster. HA! Never happened. I was so happy to have a playmate that a nearly instant love for Chuck blossomed. Aannnd … it seems as though he reciprocated quickly.

During those formative early to late teen years we became joined at the hip as they say, and had but one actual argument that whole time, and it quickly dissolved. We hunted together, rode together, took our bikes all over the countryside, skinny dipped with our close buddy Don nearly every day of the summer. When we weren't into any of those pursuits we were exploring any place we didn't think we had ever been.

Add cars to those things later on, and we did separate our activities a little bit, but not much. We had and still have a deep, abiding love and respect for one another. I claim that as a work of God, I really do. I am proud of who, what, and how Chuck is.

After Dad quit farming and became an independent builder, we did very little farming on our 65 acres. Gramps did some farming with horses for a bit, then Dad bought a little John Deere, and that became our means of tilling. (The horses stayed.) As a result of that, both Chuck and I worked for neighboring farmers and so can still claim the legacy of farming. My favorite part was baling hay because of the cool pond swim at the end of the day.

I played Babe Ruth baseball and batted lead-off every year, played left field or second base, and stole more bases than just about anyone. I played basketball, too, but was third string even though I was six feet tall by my senior year! I had grown over 5 inches during the short summer between my sophomore and junior years and lost nearly all semblance of coordination! Wow, did I ever experience embarrassment at times. That coordination would not catch up to me before Navy boot camp at age 18. I finally became the basketball player I wanted to be around the age of 22. Hey, better late than never, right?

My love for anything that flew drew me to model airplanes, and I started building them at age eight or so, still do at the ripe old age of 77. I have competed for many of those years in control line precision aerobatics, with some semblance of success, and love designing and scratch building the beasts. The flying of those actually accelerated my learning to fly the full scale airplanes when I was 31. I soloed in just 11 hours, only six of those with a certified instructor. (Bragging time.)

EXTRAORDINARY LIVES

You see, at just the right time,
when we were still powerless,
Christ died for the ungodly. 7
very rarely will anyone die for
a righteous man, though for
a good man someone might
possibly dare to die. 8 But God
demonstrates His own love for
us in this: While we were yet
sinners, Christ died for us.

Romans 5:6-8 (NIV)

Chapter Four

SHOULD TITLE THIS **"POST** school." When I graduated high school in 1958, Donna was already in college. By the time I left the Navy, she was already teaching third grade at Swanton, Ohio.

BUT - I was in hog heaven because the skinny little hillbilly boy from the foothills of the Appalachians was learning new things about airplanes, and would soon be actually working on them! I went into the Navy under a guaranteed program which assured me my choice of any school I wanted because of my high scores on the tests.

I went to boot camp in Great Lakes, Illinois, then on to aviation prep school in Norman, Oklahoma. (WHAT in the world was the Navy doing with an air base in OKLA-HOMA?!! Ain't no ocean down there!) We learned the basics in every field of Naval aviation, and then it was on to class "A" school. For me, that was aviation electronics in Memphis, Tennessee.

That schooling was eight hours a day, five days a week, and that was all electronics. What a masterful means of teaching they had! They crammed over two years of college electronics knowledge into us in 26 weeks. And I assure you, when we hit the squadrons to perform our jobs, we hit the tarmac on the run. We became very good at our tasks in a very short time. I can't brag enough on our great Navy's training schools.

A true rookie, fresh out of boot camp

While I was there I got back into the model airplane hobby and learned a lot about the different events, but concentrated on combat with the control line planes. What a blast! The base had a hobby shop and a club known as the Navy Memphis Tailhooks, and I spent way too much time there instead of studying. I got top grades in spite of that because of the incredible memory. I was later to discover the false sense of security that was giving me. When I got into a squadron, I had to spend a lot of time learning how to USE that learning and turn the memorized knowledge into PRACTICAL knowledge! Fortunately for me, there were a couple of second class petty officers who liked helping rookies.

The flight line of VS 39

I was transferred to VS-39 which was in Quonset Point, Rhode Island in October of 1959 and would finish my four-year enlistment there. VS-39 was an airborne anti-submarine squadron deployed aboard the USS Essex aircraft carrier when they were not in port in a barracks and hanger. What an adventure that was for the skinny hillbilly kid. I loved it. Yes, I did my share of the typical complaining about the military stuff, but underneath I very seriously considered making it a career. I often wonder what would have been had I done that. BUT - God had other plans for me! Wow, what He did for me!

The skipper's plane and Will

We spent equal time, almost, at sea on the ship. When on the base at Quonset, we lived pretty much a normal life with regular jobs. Once I was promoted to second class petty officer, I didn't even stand any night watches. Very nice.

We made one "Med" (Mediterranean) cruise 1960, and spent three months going to and through the Mediterranean Sea, putting into several foreign ports and getting to experience the culture differences of those countries.

We visited Lisbon, Portugal; Barcelona, Spain; Athens, Greece; went through the Suez Canal into the Indian Ocean and then made port in Karachi, Pakistan. Talk about culture shock!! It was a wonderful experience.

Back in the states we settled back into life on the base. When getting ready to return to Ohio for Christmas leave I found a ride with a shipmate as far as Columbus, Ohio, and would take a bus from there to Marietta. He drove a Jaguar XK120 and I quickly fell in love with sports cars!

When we got back from leave I went with my friend to the place where he bought the Jag' and promptly fell for a 1957 MGA! I made that my twenty-first birthday present to myself and have never looked back! I ended up racing in the slalom type "parking lot" races the next two summers and got a huge dose of incurable "sports-car-itus" that still inhabits my body, mind, and spirit! One of the biggest spiritual lessons of my life was a result of that. It will be chronicled later.

While in Quonset Point I did many of the things sailors are supposed to do; I drank some, but discovered, thankfully, that alcohol and I did not coexist very well. About the third or fourth time I woke up needing to get better in order to die I thought, "Why have I given myself the flu on purpose?!" That ended that, and from then on I would nurse one beer all night to be with the buddies. Remember, I was not yet a Christian.

****

LIFE ON THE AIRCRAFT CARRIER WAS SOMETHING this skinny hillbilly never would have thought would happen in my life . When I graduated from aviation electronics school in Memphis I was shipped to the Quonset Point NAS (Navel Air Station) and my squadron, VS39 would be deployed aboard the USS Essex for weeks at a time to patrol the east coast. The cold war was in full swing and Russia had spy submarines snooping on a regular basis. Our job was to know where they were, and to be ready for any needed action against them.

Picture the kid who had nothing but airplanes on his brain as he walked that flight deck among the real things instead of models! Being a junior guy, I was assigned to night check. (That means second shift.) But ... because of my eyes not allowing me to qualify for flight crew status, I was assigned to the CAG, or carrier air group, to repair the electronic gear and keep it in top, usable shape. I worked in a shop loaded with test equipment just one deck below the flight deck and the guys still assigned to the squadron would simply swap out a non-working piece of gear, bring it to us, claim a replacement and leave the bad unit with us. We then fixed the bad unit and had it ready for the next needed swap.

There were times when I had no gear on my bench and I would venture to the flight deck area to observe night ops. What a hubub of activity the launches were. Then I was assigned to the flight deck troubleshooting crew for a while and actually got to experience first hand the exciting operations there. Imagine yourself in the dark of night, there are six twin engine aircraft running, and the one farthest back has a radio glitch. You wend your way carefully through the darkness as you make sure where those spinning props are, all twelve of them! Now you have the problem fixed, and it's back to the side while ducking all those props again! Exciting, scary, and adrenaline pumping all describe the experience.

Let me tell a story on myself as to how I got to be on the flight deck crew, though you may never trust me again once you read it. The electronics repair shop had a lot of hours when everything was working and there were no repairs needed for anything. We usually played some cards during those times, or read, or anything else to occupy the time.

However, the chief petty officer of my squadron shop didn't like that. Nobody really understood what bugged him about it; there simply was nothing to do and we were at least in the shop in case an emergency came up. One night when he walked into the shop and I happened to be the first guy he saw with a handful of cards. We always played double pinochle, so there were a lot of them. Our CAG shop had techs from every squadron and I was the only one at the bench from mine. He jumped all over me, telling me that if he ever caught me doing that again he would pull me back to the squadron and put me on flight deck night duty for a couple of weeks.

Wait a minute now; wait just a minute. I had, only a week before, asked him if I could go on flight deck duty for that cruise. His answer was that I was too valuable in the CAG shop because of what I worked on. I was one of only two guys who had experience and success with the TACAN equipment.

My twisted little brain immediately jumped to a solution for my desire to troubleshoot the flight deck gear!! I passed the word to the guys that if they saw the chief coming toward CAG they should tell me if they had time. It so happened that he made a trip the following week and one of the guys saw him leave the squadron shop. He called and I happened to not be playing then. The tech that took the call hollered for me to grab someone's hand and set down at the bench quick. Another petty officer jumped up, handing me his cards, and when the chief walked in, guess who he saw first! Yup, I went to flight deck troubleshooting right then, laughing all the way! Behind my hand, of course. I think the chief figured it out later on, because he acted sort of sheepish around me for a while after that.

Near the end of my last cruise at sea, two other second class petty officers and I were flown off the ship and sent to Key West, Florida for special training on new solid state electronics gear. We were going be getting all new aircraft equipped with the new stuff and the differences were tremendous. We three second class guys would start the training of the rest of the shop as well as maintaining the new gear. The schools would take eleven weeks of our time. This was in the fall of 1961 and we returned to the squadron just in time for Christmas leave.

While we were there, the Navy neglected to send our pay records with us, so we were mostly broke the whole time! I had my Mom wire me some cash, but not a lot, and we really spent a lot of time at the free beaches and nursing one drink at the night spots for a whole evening. The great result of this time, however, was that I left the Navy having both the older tube theory electronics and the new solid state theory coming out for everything! What an advantage they had given me for civilian life!

Therefore, since we have been justified through faith, we have peace with God through our Lord Jesus Christ, through whom we have gained access by faith into this grace in which we now stand.

Romans 5:1 & 2 (NIV)

Chapter Five

I NEED TO RELATE THIS NEXT STORY in order to show that we need to reserve judgment on people until we really know what and who they are. That same chief petty officer in charge of the electronics shop was pretty much disliked by all. He was blustery, loud, and a real "pure Navy" kind of guy. Gung-ho is the typical term. He earned the nickname of Bullmoose when he first came to the squadron because of his mouthy presentation and gung-ho Navy preaching.

I learned one of life's most important lessons even before knowing Christ because of the chief. That lesson was to judge not, lest ye be judged.

We had just loaded the squadron aboard the Essex and put to sea for three weeks when, on the first day out, I was called to the chaplain's office below decks. I was informed that my grandpa had died and there was no way I could get off to attend the funeral. I was devastated.

When I got back up to the electronics shop the chief drew me out into the passageway and asked me what they wanted me for. When I told him, he asked if my Gramps and I were close. He could tell by my being very broken up that the answer was "Yes."

Then he asked me if I would like to get emergency leave to go home for the funeral and I said yes, but I couldn't get off the ship. He gently took me by the arm and led me below decks to the pilots' ready room, walked me right up to the commanding officer's desk and proclaimed something like this; "Captain, Hinton here was just told that he has lost his grandfather but can't get off for emergency leave because we're at sea. However, you and I know that tomorrow morning there will be a small craft with dignitaries aboard putting alongside to put them aboard the carrier. I think we should arrange for this man to be on that craft when it goes back to Quonset, don't you?"

The look on the skipper's face told me the chief wasn't supposed to know about the people coming aboard to observe the war games to be played that week, but he was a good skipper and made the arrangements. I got my emergency leave right then and there, packed my seabag, and was long gone by early morning to retrieve my MG and head for Ohio. My chief was not the hard case man most thought him to be, but a caring leader.

Chief was known for his long and persuasive "shipping over" lectures when someone was becoming a short timer. But when my time was getting near and he called me into his office at the hanger, all the guys laughed at me and told me, "He'll ship you over, Hint', you wait and see."

They were wrong, even though I had seriously contemplated a career with Uncle Sam's Navy. He looked across the desk at me and said something very close to this.

"Hinton, you're about to the end of this hitch, and I don't think you should think about shipping over. You are much too scientific minded to waste your life in a military spot because if you ship, in two years you'll be a first class petty officer and won't be using your technical knowledge any more; so you get out there and get yourself a top paying job and make a lot more money than you ever can in here."

I was out of his office in less than five minutes and the guys were convinced I had re-upped! I never told them different until a couple of days later! When it was time for that goodbye hoorah, Chief went with us and paid for all my drinks. It didn't cost him much, I'll tell you that.

****

THE MAIN REASON FOR MY NOT GOING CAREER wasn't Chief's talk. My best buddy Fred had connected me with GE in Syracuse, New York, where I was all but promised a job in their military design department. It promised to be very lucrative so I made my plans for that. That was six months before I was to be discharged. I was excited to be going to Syracuse to be close to Fred and his bride Dottie. I loved those two a lot, and we still communicate. What a blessing they are.

I was supposed to get out the middle of October in 1962, but the ship was leaving for a cruise on October first into the Caribbean. They asked me to extend for the six weeks of the cruise, but I said no to that. The yeoman took me to the skipper and suggested they let me out early, which is what happened. My original discharge date happened to be the day Kennedy blockaded Cuba! I was already in Syracuse by then. Do you see God's Hand in the events here? I surely do. Even though I had not yet accepted Christ as my Lord, He was orchestrating my path to the course He had set for me. Had I still been in the squadron they would have extended me two years automatically because I was a critical rate. That would have settled it for me; I would have gone career and would never have met Donna, my life's assignment, privilege, and blessing.

And we rejoice in the hope of the glory of God. 3: Not only so, but we rejoice in our sufferings, because we know that suffering produces perseverance.

Romans 5:2a - 4 (NIV)

Chapter Six

ALL THE TIME MY NAVY CAREER was unfolding, my future bride was feeling the call to missions. She had taken secretarial courses in high school and was working in Montpelier, Ohio as a secretary for a local plant. As she sensed the call of God on her life, she finally gave in and told her folks about that call. She enrolled at Fort Wayne Bible College and spent the next four years there.

Once she graduated she went to Livonia, Michigan for a missions internship, living with a pastor's family and doing various ministry duties while there. Part of her duties involved leading a Good News Club for Child Evangelism Fellowship involving the area youth.

As I look back at Donna's life, I have come to believe that's where she first developed her deep love for children and the teaching of them. Once she was through the internship she applied with several missions organizations. The results were much the same; since she wasn't married and also was so small, they all turned her down.

She was told by some if she could maintain 110 pounds she would be approved. HA! The only time my little lady maintained over 110 pounds was during pregnancy and after giving birth to two children!

What both Donna and I have come to realize, and truly believe, is that yours truly was to be her mission field! That's right; me, old Will Riley; the skinny hillbilly, was her mission field. (And she served there oh so very well.)

But I stray from her story again. Once Donna was back in the northwest Ohio region she became good friends with a couple in Swanton, Ohio, and was told of a teaching position there. That particular superintendent had had a few teachers from Fort Wayne Bible College and loved their work ethic and attitude, so she got the job right away. The stipulation was that she extend her education during the summers because she had never had student teaching at Fort Wayne. She did so at Bowling Green State University and ended up just a class or two from gaining her master's degree.

She rented a room from an older couple and settled in to the typical life of a third grade teacher; went roller skating during the week from time to time, made trips back to Montpelier to her folks, and just sort of blended into the local culture.

She dated a bit, always with "church" guys, and spent much of her evenings doing lesson plans in preparation for the following day's classes.

Why was this pretty, sweet teacher not married soon? Well, that takes a bit of explaining so you will see just how we came to believe God had her there for me and me there for HER. You see, Donna was told so very often as a child that she was too skinny to be healthy. That affected her personal worth thoughts tremendously and she did not think she could ever really be thought of as pretty, sexy, or attractive. As a consequence, by the time I happened on the scene, she was pretty much alone except for her teaching friends. Here's why it is important for you to understand why she and I believe God had her waiting for me.

Donna's graduation picture

I was just about as awkward with girls as a guy can be. No confidence, afraid of rejection, pretty much a loner except for my buddies. So please allow me to drop back to my story for now so I can link these two together properly.

****

WHEN I ARRIVED IN SYRACUSE, EAGER FOR MY NEW job, I discovered GE had decided to move the military design department to Arizona for tax purposes. So there I was, unemployed. After a couple of weeks I just naturally gravitated to the airport for employment and was hired immediately for the line crew because of my basic knowledge of all aircraft operations. For instance, aviation fuel is color coded by octane and is a must know. It was very basic knowledge necessary in the military. That knowledge got me the job.

The line crew is responsible for fueling, for directing incoming aircraft to a parking place, (those wings can really get in the way without guidance), putting the aircraft in the hangers at night, making sure those outside are properly tied down, and so forth.

I worked 51 hours a week, just like all the others. That consisted of five nine-hour days and one shift from midnight to six AM. Then we had two days off and started the schedule all over again.

The folks where I rented a room had also been where my Navy buddy, Fred, rented until he and Dottie were married. When he moved out they saved it for me for several weeks. Gard, the husband, was a steel guitar player in a popular country band and I soon had a lead guitar job that proved to be a good supplement to my other income.

We played everything from dives to clubs and all in between and never lacked for gigs. I thought I was on top of the world with that part of life, not realizing I was playing for the wrong one.

That winter was a corker! Syracuse is right in the path of lake effect snow and wow, did we ever get it. Plus, for three weeks in a row I got up to below zero temperatures. I had sold my little sports car and paid thirty-five dollars for a 1954 Dodge with no floorboard on the passenger's side. Whenever I hit a drift of any size, my plywood floor over there would pop up and snow would fly all over. The Dodge was to only last until spring, and each snowdrift re-cemented that thought in my mind!

The next step in my life, the one that kicked off the major life-changing events, came as a result of my job at the airport with the line crew. An aircraft came in and unloaded the executives it carried, and when the pilot was checking in at the desk I noticed they were from Toledo, Ohio.

"What kind of things are available at Toledo?" I asked.

"What are you looking for?" was his answer.

"I'm an avionics tech and there's nothing here."

He quickly wrote down a name and phone number and told me to call the man on Monday morning and tell him what I wanted and that Ed Hale said to hire me! I followed his advice and was headed for Toledo two days later.

If you'll go back and read the prologue again, you'll see why I feel this was of God's leading and purpose. He had chosen me to be Donna's life partner well in advance of this. I truly believe that and I always will.

My job with the fixed base operator at Toledo Express didn't work out as I had intended. While I was making fair money in the electronic shop, the guy running the shop and I really didn't get along too well. I was Navy, knew my stuff and did things the Navy way. He had no military time, was a local grad who did things differently and was bound and determined that's how the old sailor was gonna do them! He ran up against a brick wall because I had a nasty temper in those days and explained to him where the bear went in the woods and that he should never, ever poke the bear.

Well, I was wrong, of course, and it cost me my avionics position, but I had had to do some non avionics jobs during those first few weeks and the service manager liked my attention to detail. He kept me on as a mechanic even though I didn't have an A&P license (Airframe and Powerplant).

That's a common practice because a qualified A&P will always inspect the final work done by those not licensed. It's totally safe and above board. I actually became happier doing that than I was with the avionics work. At that time in history, aviation wasn't paying all that well, but I didn't care. I was eating three squares a day, having fun with my fellow workers, and life was good. After all, I was working on AIRPLANES!

As I watched that pretty little school teacher in the mornings at breakfast, I slowly worked up the courage to ask her out. That, dear people, was a slooooooow process because I was so paranoid over possible rejection! Then one morning as I was walking to the restaurant the rain was starting to fall just as I passed her house. She was just getting into her little VW and offered me a ride to the restaurant I accepted.

Hmmmm, was that the event that gave me the courage to ask her out? Well, not exactly, although I'm sure it bolstered my courage somewhat. Sometime in January we had a lot of overtime at the airport and I was money ahead of my expenses. Being as that was so, I finally found the courage to sit down with her in her booth at breakfast! Wow, what a breakthrough.

As I look back, I still didn't work up to asking until she had stood up and was saying goodbye! But ... I finally did, she said yes, and the wonderful journey started. I was driving a 1957 Chevy ragtop at the time, and the back window was history, so I traded 57s with my friend Gary for the date. We went to a nice spot in Toledo and then to a movie in Maumee, Ohio, titled, *Take Her, She's Mine* starring Jimmy Stewart and Sandra Dee. How about that;

I remembered. Donna never got over the fact that I could recall the specifics of that date so well, but it started a journey that would continually change my life. (And hers.)

I think we fell in love that very night, even though I was late picking her up, because I couldn't find the new address she had moved to for a while. Our second date was Sunday lunch at her place, and the third was Monday evening. Yup, we had fallen hard and I remember teasing her that night.

I said to her, "You better be careful, little lady, or I just might ask you to marry me."

"You better not."

"And why not?"

"Because I might say yes."

"Would you?"

"Yes."

As far as the two of us were concerned, the deal was struck that very moment. That conversation is a direct and accurate quote, by the way, because it has been forever etched in my mind and heart. I glow when I get to tell people I proposed on the third date and she said "Yes."

During this time together Donna had asked if we would attend church once we were married. Having gone while growing up it was no big deal for me to say "yes," so the matter was decided.

There was one day when the world almost fell in on me. Just before we started dating Donna had purchased a brand new 1963 Volkswagen bug, and because my 57

Chevy convertible had the back window out we drove the Bug whenever and wherever we went. Remember that I had raced my little MGA for a couple of summers in the autocross races? Well, this little car had nowhere near the power of my MG, but with the four-wheel independent suspension it would corner like a cannon ball rolling down a laundry chute!

Next, remember that I basically learned to drive in New England. No matter what they say about New England drivers, they are crazy to a person. If there is half a car length in the traffic, they charge right in, expecting the others to make room! Honest truth.

So ... I still drove New England style with that sweet little VW while in Toledo. We pulled into her drive one afternoon, shut the car off and Donna started sobbing, crying like someone had just died! When I asked her what was wrong she wailed out, "I can't marry you!"

Wow. I sat there dumbfounded and asked her why not, and her answer shocked me. "I won't spend the rest of my life terrified of the way you drive. I am so scared right now I could almost be sick to my stomach.

"You cut people off, you jump curbs, you drive like a maniac and I can't live like that! I am just so scared."

Well, needless to say I was shocked. I figured everybody drove like that, especially with that neat little car you could fit into unimaginable spaces! My answer was instant, more or less, and I promised to try to change.

That didn't cut it; I had to promise I WOULD change. Well, needless to say at this point in our story, I did promise and I did change. Slowly, you understand, but changed nevertheless.

One big chuckle later, much later, in our lives together was coming down a four lane south out of Toledo and turning onto another four lane going West toward Napoleon and Liberty Center. The ramp from route 23 onto route 24 had a really neat curve that just begged for a good acceleration through it and I punched that Buick

Front entrance of the church, JUST MARRIED!

Park Avenue when we swung into the turn. All of a sudden this little yell came from the right seat as she hollered, "Go, Will Riley, go!!"

I looked at her and saw a huge smile on her face as she held on tight. I guess she had, over the years, discovered my penchant for sideways G forces in a hard turn!

That wonderful wedding day!

****

WE SET A DATE FOR THAT FALL, BUT NEAR THE FIRST of June our friends told us they were going to move because of a job change and that their apartment was completely furnished, including linens and kitchen stuff, and all we needed was our clothes. We upped the date to June thirteenth.

That was almost not to happen as Donna began to be quite ill, and I finally bundled her up and took her to her

Donna and her VW by the wedding night motel

mom in Montpelier, Ohio, because I couldn't be with her enough to properly care for her. As it turned out, this little thing lost weight all the way down to 84 pounds!

The cause was finally discovered when a toothache surfaced and the dentist found an impacted wisdom tooth. Wow, was I one worried guy during that period because a classmate of mine had been built tiny like Donna, and one week before her wedding date she had died from leukemia that was discovered only one week before that. What a relief for all of us when the dentist made his discovery.

So, on June thirteenth of 1964, a 26-year-old Donna and 24-year-old Will were married in a family only wedding. My best man was my buddy Gary, whose 57 Chevy had been the magic carriage on our first date. Her maid of honor was another Donna who was her best friend most of their lives.

We had no reception; Gary and the other Donna just drove us around town in my 57 with the top down while blowing the horn a lot. After that we changed clothes, climbed into her 63 VW bug and headed out for Holland, Michigan. We only had the weekend because of my new job.

New job? What new job? Oh yes, while this engagement was going on another friend of hers gave me a lead on a much better paying job in an industrial plant. I hated the thought of leaving aviation, but the money difference was something else! Remember, this was 1964 and aviation, at least general aviation, wasn't paying what it should have. They didn't need to because most of us would have worked on airplanes for nothing if they only fed us. We were that loyal and infatuated with those magnificent flying machines.

However, I got the distinct feeling that my new bride expected to be fed three meals a day. I think this is a repeat from earlier in this story, but it still fits here. I applied for the mechanics' job as suggested, but during the interview with the head of maintenance he noticed the avionics and inquired about it. Turns out they had an opening for an industrial electrician, and asked if I might be interested in that.

He brought the electrical foreman up to check me out and I ended up taking that job. I left the aircraft mechanic job at $1.65 an hour, the top rate, for $2.32 an hour with THREE raises possible after that! That was a no brainer for me, so on June 8th of 1964 I started work at the Campbell Soup Company factory at Napoleon, Ohio.

Gotta admit, that was a real stretch for me. I hated being inside and I hated being without my contact with flying machines! The money was good, however, and the other electricians were supportive, as was my new boss. Being an old squirrel hunter, I had the patience to stick with it and ended up being there a very long time. More on that later.

During those first months I had to have been led by God, even though I was not yet a Christian, because I complimented Donna on every aspect of her being. Thing is, I meant every word and it wasn't that I knew to do that, I was just crazy with love and infatuation where this magnificent creature was concerned. In my heart, she had no flaws.

That was just what she needed to begin to boost her self image, and over the years we traded that encouraging exercise that served unintentionally to build up each other, for I was just as needy as she in that department. God knew what each of us needed and He worked through us to develop two very self-confident people as we shared our lives together. I believe with all my heart that ours WAS a match made in heaven. And such a perfect match it was.

That if you confess with your mouth, "Jesus is Lord," and believe in your heart that God raised him from the dead, you will be saved. For it is with your heart that you believe and are justified and it is with your mouth that you confess and are saved.

Romans 10:9 & 10 (NIV)

Chapter Seven

WE DIDN'T STAY AT THE Swanton apartment very long because the drive was a killer and I wanted to be closer to work. We moved to an upstairs apartment in Napoleon, Ohio after only six weeks. The previous apartment owner was very upset, and I really don't blame him, but the deed was done anyway.

Morning sickness soon invaded our lives and we drew even closer. Little Donna, as I called her for 51 years, (still do, as you can see) was quite a sight with her "baby tummy" thrusting out ahead of her, and the next year our son, Douglas, was born after 32 hours of labor! That poor girl; I still get just a bit angry with that doctor when I realize he should have done a C section long before then.

Thing is, at some point when he sent me into the hall to allow him to do an exam, I fell asleep leaning on the wall. Doc woke me up and sent me home while promising to call me as soon as he knew she was going to give birth.

I woke up just a little before 9:00 AM the next morning to the landlady from downstairs beating on our door. She told me she had heard the phone ringing off the hook for a long time in the wee hours of the morning, then they finally called her. Doug had arrived a couple of hours before that! I had fallen asleep lying across the bed fully dressed.

Now, another testament to my lack of worldly knowledge. I had no idea a hospital would let a new father in before visiting hours, so I went to church! (Big dummy.) I finally saw my wife and our new son, Douglas, around lunch time. Boy, did I feel stupid when they told me I could have gone in right away! That was a part of my early persona that God and Donna have since eliminated. What a team!

Donna developed an infection and didn't get to go home for seven days, and Doug stayed with her, of course. We settled into the new parents' role and learned all about that job together. To save Doug and me from embarrassment I won't be telling the baby stories here. Just know that we totally loved our roles as parents and figured our baby was the smartest and cutest ever born. More importantly, Donna gained her strength back fairly quickly.

We were living in an upstairs apartment then, but we began to think about a house of our own around the time Doug was six months old. One came up in Liberty Center, Ohio for a price we could afford on my income and we signed a land contract and were on our way as home owners. Doug was now nine months old.

Liberty Center is one of those rare towns and communities that just models what this country is all about, much as the town name says. People there stick together and are one of the most close-knit bunches of people you can find anywhere. I absolutely love the community, even though I've not lived there since 1996. (Once a Tiger, always a Tiger!)

The house we bought was a two-story farm house. All the adjoining lots had been part of the original tract, and our lot boasted six-tenths of an acre. That became the local touch football field, pitching practice field, and more for many years. What a joy it was for us to watch those neighborhood kids play. (Most of the time, that is.)

As Doug was approaching 21 months of age Donna suggested if we wanted more children we should get with it, because two years separation was pretty much the ideal spacing. Hey, what did I know about such things? As a result, Beth was born two years and six months to the day after Doug's birthday.

But wait! There's a huge chunk of life in between that time!! Just maybe the most important section of my personal life.

****

MY JOB WAS GOING JUST FINE, WE HAD THIS WONderful little guy who followed dad everywhere he went, the cars were running fine, Donna was pregnant, and life was wonderful.

We had continued going to church in Napoleon and the Sunday school leaders had asked me to teach a sixth grade boy's class because no one could keep them corralled. Shucks, why not, I thought?

Well, this not-yet-saved hillbilly took over that class, and those little guys learned what it meant to cross that skinny dude at the front of the class. The two mischief leaders were really cutting up the second week and I stopped the class, escorted them next door to the girls' class and asked the pastor's wife if they could sit in with the girls so they could see how they were supposed to act during class.

Well, she allowed as how they might already have the idea just from looking in right then, she suggested I please let them try again in their own class. Mission accomplished. Not a one ever tried to disturb the class again. Sit with girls at that age?! No way!

As a result of that notoriety one of the ladies of the women's group approached me with a request. The group had an annual tea in the spring and an elderly gentleman always gave a book report for them as their program. Problem was, he had committed to a mission trip during that time so they had no program scheduled. Would I consider doing the book review?

Hey, I had been on stage most of my life and thrived on it, so my answer was, "You betcha!" They gave me the book, which was *God's Warrior* by F. Slaughter and was a historical fiction work on the life of the apostle Paul. You should read it because it is excellent writing.

The night came when I had finished it, had all my notes organized on a legal pad and was ready to just settle in to rehearsing it. Donna, being just a little bit pregnant, (eight months) had gone to bed and was sound asleep. I shut down the house and slipped into the bedroom, placing the legal pad on my dresser, undressed and got in bed.

Donna was on her right side with her back to me and I got on my left side, closed my eyes, and called on sleep to come. Ha! God had other ideas. Out of the blue, no warning, no apparent reason, I began to weep. Not just weep, but sobbing! I have no idea how long that lasted, but remember worrying about waking Donna and being confused as to what was going on with me.

Then the weeping and sobbing stopped just like it had started, like a switch was flipped. I rolled over to my sleeping wife; you know, the one I was worried about waking, and took her by the shoulder. She woke, and asked me what I wanted.

My answer shocked us BOTH. I said, "Honey, I'm saved." That was the moment our wonderful God chose to expose to me the gospel of Christ's desire to be my personal Savior! Even though I was raised in a little country church and couldn't remember when I didn't believe about God, Jesus, and the like, no one had ever set me down and explained that I should AND COULD have a personal relationship with Him. I knew it at that moment! I had been shown the gospel truth by the Holy Spirit and was, at that moment, drafted into the army of God.

But seek first his kingdom and his righteousness. and all these things will be given to you as well.

Matthew 6:33 (NIV)

Chapter Eight

WOW, WHAT A NIGHT! WE sat up talking for who knows how long, wondering if I would be called to the ministry, or what would come next. Naturally, Donna was just as excited as I was because now she had that husband who believed the way she did.

God had mercy on both us and those who might have ended up in a congregation over which I would have been a pastor; He did not call me to that ministry! Of course, HE knew I do not have the tools for being a pastor. I could go on for several pages explaining the talents and personality traits I DON'T have for that high calling, but let me just say it wouldn't have been a good fit.

I'll never forget that next morning at work. As I drove the nine miles I prayed the whole route, something that would become a habit for me for the next 30 plus years. Then, when I hit the area where I was the assigned troubleshooter, I rushed to my best buddy and told him I had been saved the night before.

He'd had some bad experiences as a youngster with a certain church and looked me in the eye with this, "Now you've got your work cut out for you," and turned away. His tone of voice told me he didn't want to hear any more.

Years later he would accept Christ and become a giant as a Sunday School teacher, but that was the work of the Holy Spirit. I was so pumped that I didn't let that burst my bubble; I spent the day trying to convert the whole department! I intended to change the world in a week! Wow, did I ever get an education.

God showed me His sense of humor right away. The main follow up counselor I had was a Jehovah's Witness! He challenged me every time I opened my mouth, so I would go home and hit the scriptures to check things out. Between that and Donna's great knowledge and help, my growth was rather steady for many weeks. How I praise Him for that, for it saved me from a lot of potential trouble.

Then two wonderful Christian brothers entered my spiritual life at about the same time. They were not only brothers in Christ, they were both electricians, same as me. Junior and Russ became my very long-time mentors in the faith, and how I so love and cherish their memories and friendship. They have both "graduated" now, the term both liked to use for the transfer to heaven from this life, but I shall never forget them and the love and honesty they gave me. Believe me, neither one ever hesitated to challenge me on anything whatsoever in my life.

We had so much fun and joy for so many decades.

We took break and lunch together for most of those decades, and the bond of friendship was as strong as any band of brothers ever had. Any of the three of us would have given all we had for the other two. That bond was to show God's strength and blessings to the company many, many times over the next years, and God's presence was felt through the "trio" of fighters. More on that later.

One of the first, and most important things they taught me was that the Holy Spirit needed to have been talking to someone before I attacked them with the gospel; otherwise I was just blowing smoke as far as the recipient of my testimony was concerned. I learned to discern His guiding hand in my witnessing as a result, and the exercise of drawing people to the Savior became a real and effective part of my life. I am now, and always will be, ever so grateful for His blessing me with that gift. All the glory is HIS.

****

I MET WITH THE ENEMY'S FIRST ATTACK THE VERY first Sunday after my salvation experience. I couldn't wait to tell our pastor that morning. As circumstances would have it, he was standing outside the entrance as we walked up! I almost ran up to him and expressed my news exuberantly. He crushed me. When I had finished, he spoke these words as he turned away from me to walk into the church; "Well, a lot of people have religious experiences." His manner was one of disdain and I know my mouth must have been hanging wide open in unbelief. We started church shopping the next week!

We found our worship home the very next week at Liberty Chapel EUB church out in the country. What a wonderful bunch of people they were, and we were soon growing in His Word. We would be there 17 years until the Lord had need of us in another place. He called us out and, true to His love, sent us to another equally wonderful group of believers at Pettisville Missionary Church in Pettisville, Ohio. It was a 19-mile drive, but if God sends you, He also supplies the vehicles and gas money to do His will. Best be where He wants you.

****

OUR FAMILY LIFE IN LIBERTY CENTER WAS ABSO-lutely fantastic as a couple with kids. Kids? Plural? Yep. Less than two months later our little baby girl arrived on the scene, and God showed me His first "big" miracle. Donna had suffered through 32 hours of labor with Doug, and I had been praying like a solder on a mission for that not to be with the next baby. He was gracious, and my little 5'2" bride, who normally only weighed 110 pounds, barely made it to the delivery room for that next, and final, family member. Yep, Beth arrived with less than an hour of labor! God was so very good to us, and Donna pointed out that He was responsible for the change. She was so wise in His ways.

Now the Hintons were about to settle into the ideal

suburban lifestyle with Dad going to work, Mom cooking, cleaning, and mothering. The kids, of course were doing those growing children things that delight parents. Sound like a start to a typical Midwestern, Bible belt family existence? HA! Remember, Donna and I were both Christians now, and God had other plans for our family's lifestyle. Great plans. Exciting plans. Blessed plans.

The life as a dad was wonderful; our little guy went every where Dad went, and there was never a doubt as to whether or not that was to happen. If I started for the door, here he came on the run. I loved it. And that little girl? We about wore out a rocking chair together. There is no more joy than raising kids for Jesus when He is directing you.

The Hinton family - kids are 8 and 6.
Note the hippy hair on Will.

During those years Donna and I found another common interest in the form of music. She had a good alto voice which blended well with my tenor and we both loved southern gospel music. With me playing an acoustic guitar as accompaniment we began to sing at area churches for their evening services or their week-long evangelistic services.

We would only do one night at the latter, of course, but we had a great time doing so and it drew us even closer together. Those days are quite amusing to me now as I look back at them. Those were the times when "show people" really dressed loud. No, no, not SANG loud, but DRESSED loud. I had bright red, powder blue, and bright green sport coats. Hey, we went in style! I really don't remember just how many years we sang together, but long enough to have it be very rewarding as a couple leading worship.

As our children grew we were eased into other spiritual positions, and when they were around ten and eight we became youth leaders of the church. That lasted five years, until our own kids were getting to the youth group age when we decided it was time to quit for a couple of reasons. First, we were getting burned out, and second, we didn't feel it wise to be the leaders for our own children.

Donna was a stay-at-home mom until Beth reached the age of six, although she did some substitute teaching during the school year. Then the local superintendent approached her about teaching full time at the Liberty

Center school in the fourth grade. After praying about it for couple of days, she felt it was the right thing to do and accepted the position. Life quickly became more interesting!

My girl was a dedicated teacher. During the school year she would spend anywhere from two to three hours on lesson plans and other school work in the evening as she prepared for the following day. That never changed from the early 70's until 1989, when she was forced to quit because of her eyesight. You have to wait for an explanation of that, but take heart, it's coming and is the basis for God's most exciting working in our lives.

In 1972 the high school burned to the ground in a fire that remained unsolved. As a result, the high school classes moved into the elementary building, which was unscathed, and the elementary grades scattered out to area churches and other available buildings that opened their doors. I told you this is a great community!

Donna taught her fourth grade in our own church's basement and the next two years actually went fairly smoothly.

After a couple or so years at that level, a first grade position opened up and little Donna found her niche! What a love she had for those first graders every year! I thought she was enjoying her life before, but that was nothing compared to those first-grade years. They were to be hers for the rest of her career.

Trust in the Lord with all your heart and lean not on your own understanding. In all your ways acknowledge him and he will make your paths straight.

Proverbs 3:5 & 6 (NIV)

Chapter Nine

DURING THIS TIME WE SAW God's hand in a lot of things in our lives, including my work. I had been serving in various areas during the first four years at the plant when my foreman called me into his office and told me he wanted me to take over the troubleshooter position in the sterilizing, labeling, and palletizing area. It was a maze of conveyors that were automated for when and where they sent the canned soup and/or the full cases of same; it also had automatic palletizers, huge hydrostatic sterilizers, and a ton of other electronically controlled goodies.

I was thrilled because it was the best area in the plant and included some really complex equipment. I finally felt I was using my electronics training and experience. I was to remain there for nearly 25 years, and if I had to be in an industrial surrounding, that was the best place. I had my own shop, and after a couple of years of hard work, had accurate and up-to-date prints.

During those years I would serve under several different production supervisors in charge of that production area and each one had, of course, his own approach to getting things done. Some were great, more than a couple were totally clueless, and those were the ones I felt made me become a babysitter as to what problem needed to be solved next. My boss had my back every time, and life was okay as far as being an industrial electrician.

Once I gave my life to Christ, life became more interesting. Not long after I started reading the Scripture, I was convicted about working the Lord's day. After some prayer and discussion at home, I walked into the foreman's office and informed him I would no longer be working any Sundays.

THAT went over like a lead balloon! Thing was, I could tell he wanted there to be no chance whatsoever of losing me, and his final comment was the fact that he would have to charge me the overtime anyway. We had a balanced overtime process so no one could get more OT hours than any of the others on the crew. Shoot, that didn't bother me, go with it. After all, the balance was in effect because most WANTED overtime (OT).

That decision was to give many opportunities for God to show His mighty hand down through the years I was there. Thing is, my two mentors I told you about before came to the same decision at that time and joined me in the stand. That made three electricians who wouldn't work the Lord's day.

Several years later things came to a head and the other electricians, (who wanted all the OT they could get) decided we needed to be forced to work Sundays. I still chuckle at that. We had a day crew meeting in the office that became quite energetic. One of the most humorous things during that was this: I told the loudest complainer that he, too, could refuse Sundays just like we were. If he wanted that freedom, all he had to do was have the courage to stand up for his right.

He quickly responded to the foreman that, from then on, he would work no more Sundays! As the discussion went on I could see him come to the realization of what he had done. He was perhaps the person wanting the most OT he could get, and there he was, refusing a double time day! Talk about watching a loud mouth squirm, I about laughed out loud.

He finally "took pity" on the boss and relented out of "the goodness of my heart." It was sweet the way the Holy Spirit put the right words in mine, Junior's, and Russ's mouths at just the right time and nearly two dozen day shift electricians left the office with their tails between their legs.

It was interesting to note that the three of us were regarded as some of the top troubleshooters on the crew. Our skills could not be questioned so that never entered into the discussions.

Oh well, enough on that for now, more later on this same subject, because it reared its ugly head many times in many different ways but God never failed to guide and bless us.

****

THREE OTHER GOOD FRIENDS AND I WERE FLYING model airplanes a lot from 1965 or '66 until the early '70s, and that activity occupied a big chunk of my time with building as well as flying. My interest actually grew more than ever before in spite of a bit of a time crunch created by being a family man; and I began to fly competition with a vengeance. That would continue until 1971.

Remember the penchant I had for watching any airplanes flying over? Donna, bless her heart, noticed that, and one day while on state route 109 headed toward Delta, Ohio. I was tracking a Piper Tri-Pacer through the windshield when she asked me, "Why don't you take our income tax return and go get your flying license?"

Oh, my. What a big dog that girl turned loose with that suggestion. I told her I would do that on one condition, that we buy our own plane later on because we would never be able to use the license much if we didn't. After explaining the possibilities of doing that and the prices of the currently available small planes, she agreed and thought it would be great to be able to make longer weekend trips in our own plane.

I talked to my good friend Alva, another electrician, about it, and he offered to get me started in his airplane for just the fuel cost. He and his son Gale, who would later

74

Our first airplane, a Tri-Pacer

become a business partner, owned a Piper Pacer.

I agreed and started the next week. It was nearing spring time and we encountered a few snow flurries from time to time, but in a couple of weeks or so we had put in six hours together in spite of the weather. Alva then told me he had me as far along as he, a private pilot, could take me and I should find a licensed instructor.

As life would have it, I went to a little grass strip just outside of Delta, Ohio and signed up for lessons in that same Tri-Pacer that had started the whole thing! Just five hours of instruction later I soloed. You can think anything you want, but there were two things that entered into my soloing so quickly. One, my involvement in and love for aviation and my being so familiar with airplanes, and two, as would later come out with every instructor I ever flew with, God had/has gifted me with the natural ability. On my way to a commercial pilot's license, an instructor rating, an instrument rating, an instrument instructor's rating, a multi-engine rating, and last but not least, an agriculture certificate, every last instructor I flew with made comment numerous times concerning my abilities in the cockpit. Please don't take this as bragging. I am simply stating that God definitely had His Great hand in it. All glory goes to Him.

This is a bit ahead of my story, but seems to fit here. I soloed in April of 1971, got my private license in September, and figured that was it. God had other plans. During my morning drive to work, those nine miles were my prayer time to start the day. I had learned about MAF (Mission Aviation Fellowship) even before I started flying myself, and prayed often for them. At a stop sign one morning as I did so, the Holy Spirit spoke to me that He wanted such a service stateside for missionaries who needed transportation while home on leave. Before I reached work several minutes later I even had the title, Missionary Shuttle Service, in mind.

I said to Him, "I can't do it. I would have to have a commercial license for that and there is no way we can afford that." Ha! Forgot Who I was talking to, didn't I?

I did tell Donna about what I felt was a call from Him, but we agreed it was way out of our reach. Ha again. I had signed up for a commercial drafting course under the

GI bill, then decided sitting at a drafting board all day simply was way out of my wheelhouse. I had dropped it and assumed that wasted my GI bill benefits.

That weekend her older brother, a career Army dude, "just happened" to drop in on his way somewhere. He had never been to our place in all the years we had been married, (seven by then), and somehow the conversation turned to the GI bill. I told him I had wasted it, and he informed me casually that I had one change of program left to my benefits.

The next Monday I stopped at the VA office in Napoleon, Ohio to check on that and left with the paperwork clutched in my taut little fist for a flying program! I went to the company where I had worked at the Toledo Express Airport and signed up, started my instruction right away, and a few months later qualified for my commercial license.

The desire to instruct had bitten me by then and I started my course for that rating. At that time, you could get the commercial license without an instrument rating, and also the basic instructor's rating. That changed a very long time ago.

Not long after I passed the instructor's check ride, my friend, Gale, had been approached to be the airport manager at the new Henry County Airport just outside of Napoleon, Ohio. The strip had been under a lawsuit for five years and that was finally settled so the commissioners were eager to get things under way.

Gale approached me about starting a flight training

school for him and I was anxious to do just that, so Henry County Flight Training was established using the very Tri-Pacer I had learned to fly in. Gale and I had purchased the beast, put a new engine in it that he had on hand, and painted it.

A lot of water went under the bridge during those first few months and we put the "Tripe" up for sale after buying a Cessna 150 for the school. The Tri-Pacer was just too noisy and costly to operate for our purpose while the 150 was the ideal training platform. If I were to begin again at this time in my life these many decades later, I would probably get another 150.

As the school grew quickly God still wouldn't let go of the MSS thing in my head and heart. I had shared it with Gale, but he couldn't see how it might work and wasn't interested. During a conversation with him about it, one of my students, Randy, listened in, asked a few questions, and then went on home.

A few days later Randy called and asked if he and Chris, his wife, could come over to the house for a visit. The answer was "Sure" and they arrived shortly after the call was over.

Randy had shared my vision with Chris; they had prayed about it and were feeling God's call to join in my dream call! We held a discussion well into the evening and when that was over, we had decided to purchase an airplane for the service that would double, or triple, as a family plane for both of our families. The search began the next day and God soon put a Cessna 172 in our path.

We had flown to look at a couple of others, but they just weren't the right ones. 8514U turned out to be the one. Randy and I flew to a place just over the Mississippi line near Memphis and made the commitment. We had all of our ducks in a row so could fly the 172 home that night. Randy got a lot of very good night experience as well as "hood time" on the way home. He would finish his private license in his own airplane.

We started the quest for a 501(c)3 rating (non-profit status) with the IRS right away; a Napoleon lawyer volunteered his services for that, and things were progressing

Our second plane, a Cessna 172,
used for mission flights

really fast. Fast, that is, until we were refused by the IRS! We ended up with Randy, Gale, and a little dynamite lady Christian lawyer from Columbus, Ohio flying to Washington to meet with the IRS.

The ineptness of some bureaucrats was sad to see when their only reason for refusing was that Randy and I were using our personally owned airplane for the service which meant we could make personal profit by doing so. That went down the tubes, I was told, in a stupendous crash when the little lady lawyer pointed out that we were leasing the aircraft to MSS for one dollar a year. I guess she really dressed them down to the point that Gale and

MISSIONARY SHUTTLE SERVICE, INC.

(A Non-Profit Corporation)
ROUTE 1, BOX 103
LIBERTY CENTER, OHIO 43532

WILL HINTON   (419) 533-4705

The business card for MSS.

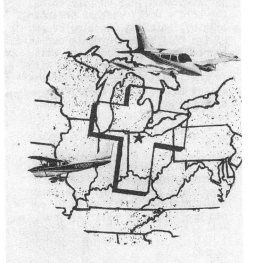

MISSIONARY

SHUTTLE

SERVICE

"For we preach not ourselves,
but Christ Jesus the Lord;
and ourselves your servants
for Jesus' sake."

(II Corinthians 4:5)

-a unique travel service
for a special people-

The front of the MSS brochure.

Randy were afraid she would make them so mad they still wouldn't let us have the rate. They signed it then and there, and MSS was on the way.

We started spreading the word around locally, then expanded that, and within a couple of months we had our first trip. I had Randy make it with me for the experience and the cross country training. He was nearly done with his private pilot training and that trip helped fill in a lot of his needs as far as hours and such. It also showed him what an aircraft being loaded to the max flew like. Another few pounds and we would have had to sit and run a few gallons of fuel off before being legal!

That taught me to ask a lot of questions when booking a trip. The gentleman said it would be him and his young son plus two small suitcases. HA! First of all, he had gone to college on a football scholarship as a lineman; second, his "young son" was around twelve and was following in Daddy's footsteps as far as build; and the final straw, one of the suitcases contained copies of the book he had published! Heavy was the word!

I told Randy he might end up hanging around the terminal for a couple of hours as I made the trip alone. But..., when I accelerated down the runway the trusty old Skyhawk lifted off like a trooper and Randy got to put in some more dual time in the left seat. Missionary Shuttle Service's first trip was a success and would kick off many more.

During those years, God put us in touch with three other similar flying services who were the same size as we were. We met with them in Pittsburg to sort out the best means by which we could coordinate our services. That meeting was beneficial to all, then He put me in contact with a gentleman out of Florida who was flying full time for God transporting medical supplies into Haiti.

The next few years were very rewarding for MSS and it was such a pleasure to be serving in that manner. Another lesson learned during those first couple of years came when I was unexpectedly asked to speak at a Sunday evening service in Findlay, Ohio. The pilot flying into Haiti called and told me he was coming to Findlay to pick up two treadle sewing machines from a large church there and planned to drop into Henry County so we could meet eye to eye. That happened, and Don spent the night at the Hintons' and went to our church the next morning.

I delivered him back out to the airport and we said our goodbyes and watched him take off for Findlay. Gale had met us there and looked at me, said we should drive down to that church to support Don, and we quickly agreed to do so.

Keep in mind that we were very conservative Christians and somewhat sheltered by our churches' conservative values. Neither of us had been exposed to the Pentecostal ways of worship or personal beliefs. I don't remember ever being conscious of the tongues movement, or baptism by the Spirit as practiced in their churches and lives.

83

The church in Findlay was very large, with a typical Sunday morning congregation of around three thousand. When Gale and I walked in that afternoon there were close to a thousand worshippers there, and at least a couple hundred at the altar praying.

We chose seats about halfway back and at the end of a pew, but Don happened to see us. We met and shared our support for him. He was just overwhelmed that we would come for his support. Not long after that, a gentleman came back to us and introduced himself as the head elder and asked us to sit up front with Don, the pastor, and the elders for the opening worship service.

Well, not much we could do but comply. I was set down right next to the pastor and we had a nice chat about MSS and our relationship with Don. Then the worship started and we all stood to sing. They had an orchestra; not just a worship team, but an orchestra! That song leader took off with Christian praise songs and we never stopped between any of them, but had seamless music going upward.

Then came a big and very valuable lesson from God. I watched as people raised their hands, some one, others both, and there was an occasional dance out in the aisle in time with the music.

I knew NOTHING of this style of worship and became quite uncomfortable with where I was. Then God SPOKE to me. He asked, "Why are you frightened of My people?" I'm serious, it happened.

At that moment I knew these people had a deep faith

and love of God that I had not yet garnered. Did I receive the gift of tongues right then? No, nor have I. But I now recognize the gift as valid, and I have long since learned to absolutely love my Pentecostal brothers and sisters! I also slowly grew into the practice of praising God during worship and when I'm alone by raising my hands to Him. When those glory bumps raise on my arms and the back of my neck, these long slender arms go high.

I am so grateful that God still speaks to us if we listen for His voice, and, in my case, sometimes when I'm NOT listening!!

*We all, like sheep, have gone
astray, each of us has turned to
his own way; and the Lord has
laid on him the iniquity of us
all.*

Isaiah 53:6(NIV)

*For the wages of sin is death,
but the gift of God is eternal life
in Jesus Christ our Lord.*

Romans 6:23 (NIV)

Chapter Ten

OUR LIVES HAD SORT OF SET-tled in to an actual family-style routine in spite of my time spent at the airport with students. I had the privilege and fun of coaching little league baseball, with Doug on my team, along with some of his best friends, and Donna and I remained active in the church. We did slip away from the singing gigs, but that was the matter of a time crunch, as I'm sure you could have guessed. I'm sure that was also a relief for the kids, since it freed them from losing evenings to our gigs.

I was approaching a crisis situation in my life that was of my own making. For as long as I could remember all I had wanted to do was be a pilot. Now I had not only achieved the privilege to fly, but was a commercial pilot!! And an instructor!! I loved instructing more than any-thing I had ever had the chance to do.

As time went on, pride got a very firm hold on me, and I slowly gave in to the feeling that I should be full time aviation. Hey, I'm a commercial pilot!! What in blazes am I doing working in a "lowly" factory?! Never mind that God hadn't told me to change anything.

I looked things over and decided the best way for me to leave the factory was to go into agricultural flying. (Crop dusting to most.) Did I pray about it? NO. But I did research the possibilities thoroughly. I really did, and decided there was a possible future in it. Donna was quite reluctant and that should have clued me in! But, with my persuasion, she finally gave in.

It would have worked fine from a business standpoint had I simply left the factory and gone totally into it, but I stayed there "just 'til the business is in the black." Just how stupid can a fellow with at least average intelligence be, for crying out loud?

I took a week's vacation and enrolled in a school up in Three Oaks, Michigan for the ag certificate. It was in the winter so we kidded about spraying for snow bugs, and it went fairly well. However, we got snowed out midway in the week and I ended up coming back home on either Wednesday or Thursday. That should have given me a clue, don'tcha think?

During this time, I started having some rapid heartbeat problems. Another clue? The problem was medically referred to as PAT, and my rate would jump to more than 200 beats a minute in an instant. Just like flipping on a switch. I would lie on my back and breath as slowly and deeply as I could and eventually it would stop, again like flipping a switch. But HURT? You bet it hurt.

Now, think this over, okay? Commercial pilot. Heart problem. Taking on more stress. WHAT IN THE

WORLD WAS I THINKING!? Pride, just plain pride, had a solid grip on me and I was bound and determined absolutely nothing was going to stop me.

Probably the most embarrassing thing I did was during my second week at Three Oaks. I had completed all my requirements for the school, was waiting on some paperwork and ready to fly back home. I sat down on a couch in the lobby and just as I did, the PAT hit me. I was really hurting big time, could barely get to the restroom I was so dizzy and in such pain. I stayed in there until it finally dropped off. I managed, barely, to get back out to the office when my instructor gave me all my paperwork and shook my hand. I was done.

After the proper goodbyes I made my way out to the Cherokee I had rented from Gale. I don't remember why I had to take it instead of the Skyhawk, but I filed an instrument flight plan to get out of the area with the snow that had started and took off.

Once I popped out of the storm into clear weather, I went brain dead. I actually set my course, set the auto pilot, and went to sleep. That doesn't even deserve an exclamation point it was so stupid. But...I was so out of it physically that the brain was also disabled.

I woke up about half an hour to forty five minutes later, plotted my location, and completed the flight VFR. (Visual Flight Rules) Back at Henry County I serviced the aircraft, tied it down, and made my way into the little terminal to sit down. Good thing I did, because the old PAT hit me again for five or so minutes.

Why in the world would a supposedly normally intelligent individual go ahead with the plans to buy the crop duster airplane and go ahead into business when he knew the FAA would suspend his medical certificate as soon as they found out? As I look back, I shake my head and wonder what would have been had I used my head instead of my backside to think with. Wow, just how blind can a person be?

I sprayed for two seasons, fighting the PAT from time to time before reality set in and I finally developed an attack of common sense! I was running a business that basically put fires out for farmers out of a pay phone in the hallway of the factory! Donna would get a call, send me a message via the maintenance secretary to call home and I would then make the necessary call to the customer.

I finally realized this was a life of sin for me. I was shirking my duties as a husband, father, and employee for the sake of following a false dream. Had I sought the Lord whether or not to go into the crop dusting I am 100% sure He would have told me "No." Truth be told, I was also avoiding my duties as the chief pilot for MSS because I was handing off most of the flights to Randy or Gale, but I was the only instrument rated pilot at that time so should have been the one making most of the flights.

Twenty-twenty hindsight flies once again. I dropped the ag business and put everything up for sale. All of the support equipment sold quickly because I had purchased good equipment; but the airplane took eight months to sell, and we ended up losing a ton of money at the time. It amounted to approximately a year's wages for me.

A beautiful thing happened about a week after we knew the total crash results of the financial situation. I came home from that hated factory job one day and was met at the top step into the kitchen by my little lady. She put her arms around me and whispered in my ear, "Things are going to be fine and wonderful and I love you."

Talk about reinforcement at a critical time! That was maybe the most needed comfort I had ever had at that point in my life. God was so faithful to us. I had confessed my sins and He had forgiven, pointed the way He intended for me, and within three years we were out of all debts except for the house payment! And we never went hungry or barefooted! Only through God could that have happened.

There was an incident with MSS after I was grounded that simply cannot be left out! Gale had come around to believing in the concept and was making a lot of trips for us. He called me at work one day in something of a panic. (A mild one.) He had been called with a request for us to pick a young lady up at Chicago O'Hare airport and transport her to her former home in Michigan.

She had been a missionary in Africa, was bitten by some exotic bug and nearly died, and had spent the last year in Holland in a hospital there. She was being flown into O'Hare by Dutch KLM airlines and needed the smaller plane transportation on the final leg home.

Gale was sure we would never get permission to fly the little six place Piper Lance into O'Hare! At that time it was the busiest airport in the world. I told him to call the FAA flight service station and get the phone number for O'Hare FAA tower, call them, and explain the need.

I got a frantic call back some half hour later from him and I thought he would crawl right through the phone. He not only had secured a flight assignment with permission to enter their airspace, but was given the call code of "Mercy One." He was to call them when he entered the control zone there and use that call instead of the aircraft number, the normal procedure.

When he called upon entering the control zone many miles out, he was cleared to land!!! O'Hare put all incoming jets into holding patterns and cleared that little six passenger plane in ahead of them. As soon as he landed a truck met him out on the runway and led him into a parking area off from the terminal and signaled him to shut down.

As soon as Gale exited the plane a security truck roared up and screamed at him to get out of there, he couldn't park that little airplane there! A gentleman pulled up in a big black car, spoke to the security guard while showing him credentials, and a very irate security guard drove away.

As that was happening, the KLM passenger jet pulled up beside him, and the girl was brought down the stairs on a stretcher and loaded, along with her nurse, into the Piper Lance from the tiny Henry County Airport. Wow, what a trip.

But wait, that wasn't all. The guy with the black car and the credentials told Gale to call ground control as soon as he was ready and still identify himself as "Mercy One." When Gale called in, he was cleared to the active runway, instructed to go around all the planes lined up on the taxi ways, and CLEARED FOR TAKE OFF!

God takes care of His people whether they are a pilot of a small mercy flight or a missionary girl on her way home for recuperation or BOTH.

Gale left us for heaven several years later due to cancer, but he never failed to mention his one and only flight into Chicago O'Hare with a Piper Lance.

****

I HAVE SORT OF SKIPPED AHEAD OF THE ACTUAL chronological order of much of those early Christian years, but it seemed to flow that direction so I have gone with it. Writing this is hard for several reasons; for one, it hurts to relive the attacks of stupidity, for another, my Donna is gone; and finally, I'm not sure what things to include and leave out. What will bore you, what is important, etc... Well, there is one event that needs to be covered for sure, and that is the 1971 or 1972 Bill Glass Crusade in Defiance, Ohio.

During a conversation at work with some believers, a mechanic brother stated that Youth For Christ had secured a Bill Glass Crusade for the following summer.

God might just as well have shouted aloud to me, for I knew in an instant that He wanted me to sell completely out to that event.

Not only did I sell out, but a few of my other brothers joined in the effort. We took part in every preparation and the like that we could. Just prior to that happening I had noticed a young man leaving his third shift job at the plant. He stood out to me because he wore a grin you could not have removed even surgically at all times. I thought he must be a brother in Christ.

Turns out that was the case, because we met at the first men's meeting for counselor training for the crusade and have been great friends ever since. There are two reasons I need to tell you Les's story - the first being that while we were waiting seated together at the first night of the crusade he jabbed my shoulder and pointed saying, "Will! Just look at that redhead!! She is beautiful!"

What poor Les failed to know was that the redhead was one of my best friends from my church. Her family and the Hintons had spent much time together, plus Becky and her sister, Robin, had baby-sat for our kids.

I blew Les's mind right then because I grabbed his arm, pulled him to his feet and said, "Let's go meet her!" That poor guy! He became terrified at what it seemed I was about to do by introducing us to a perfect stranger! We got to Becky and I introduced them properly, and while poor Les was trying to overcome being tongue-tied because of the shock, Becky smiled and talked like she and

I knew each other. Ha, we did.

Best part of this story, Les and Becky are still married all these years later. And I still love them oh so very much.

Later, when our dear friend Les pulled his '66 MGB into our Liberty Center driveway and offered it to me for a couple hundred dollars under the going price I jumped on it like a duck on a Junebug. Having had my MGA and loving it, this was an instant decision.

I drove it a while, then overhauled the engine and painted it red. Drove it a bit more and then decided a complete restoration was in order. I started tearing it down and when I got through doing so there were not two parts that had been bolted together that were still touching each other.

I spent a total of three years on that thing, and during those years I even tore the total interior out, including the dash! I built a new dash and console out of walnut, including building a new steering wheel out of the same walnut. It was exquisite, even if I do say so myself.

Once the engine overhaul was done (also by me) I got it completely together and began driving it. Drove it another eight years or so, until my world caved in again. People had been urging me to enter it into car shows and the like, but I had no desire to do that. However, that really built up my pride in the gorgeous little beast.

One summer day in 1988 I had washed it, lowered the top, and was just walking around my clean little masterpiece when, on the third trip around the Holy Spirit dropped the bomb on me. I had stopped just in front of the driver's side front fender when He spoke to me and said, "You're worshipping your car."

I had never felt the world fall on me quite like that ever before. My heart plummeted and I felt hot and cold and .....wow, what a horrible feeling. He was right!! My pride had sneaked up on me and grabbed me by the heart again!

Now, God did NOT tell me to sell the car then, but I knew in my heart of hearts that I needed to do that for my own cleansing. I vowed to myself that I would do just that.

HA! Took me a whole year to work up the courage to advertise it. But I finally did. It sold rather quickly and when that college lad turned right out of our driveway I walked into the garage and sobbed deeply for an interminable amount of time. Donna and the kids had gone to Toledo for some reason and I was glad they weren't there to see what a mess I was for quite a while. I was there among the tools and lifts and engine stand and beams and all the other special equipment and tools needed for such a project, and all of those "riches" seemed to jeer at me. It broke my heart, which needed to happen.

That taught me such a valuable lesson about material things, a lesson I have never forgotten which has guided my life from that 1989 experience to now as I write this in 2018. The first experience after that was the sale of my 1957 Les Paul Special electric guitar. I bought that instrument when I was 18 at my Mom's urging. It was supposed to be a family heirloom, ya know. I had always been very proud of that guitar, until after the MG, that is.

When our Christian contemporary band Shalom broke up in 1982 I put the guitar away and did not touch it for many years. Not a good thing, I admit, but it happened. When I saw an ad in the paper seeking vintage instruments I called the number and discovered an old friend who had gone into the vintage guitar business. In fact, he had attended every one of Shalom's concerts and had tried to buy my guitar at the end of every one.

The band "Shalom" in concert

I sold him the instrument for ten times what I had paid for it all those years ago and shed not on tear or had one second of remorse at any level; it was a piece of wood and only a piece of wood. They made new guitars every day.

I now tell people I will sell anything and everything I have but the wife and pets. And I mean it. Make me an offer.

****

THERE'S ANOTHER CHAPTER TO OUR STORY WITH Les and Becky. A couple of years after they were married, they visited our church again, (they had moved away to jobs), and during that visit they encouraged Donna and me to check out the Navigator's two-seven series. It was/ is based on Colossians chapter two, verse seven, which says, "Rooted and built up in Him, strengthened in the faith as you were taught, and overflowing with thankfulness."

The course at that time was a two year discipleship course and required instructors to take a weekend course to qualify to lead it. I took it on my own, Donna stayed behind to care for the home stand, and I started a course at church a short time later. What a wonderful time we had; learning and memorizing sixty passages of scripture during the time, sharing prayer exercises, Bible study, witnessing techniques, and many other great discipling tasks. My pastor even took it and became a true advocate of it, which led to doing a second course a few years later.

That course has since been restructured into a series of six week classes and is still a solid course for discipling people and helping them form spiritual habits in their lives such as daily scripture reading and study, daily prayer times, being prepared always to "give an answer to the hope that lies within you." (First Peter.)

Les and Becky have retired now and moved back to this area and when I find myself needing a break from the drudgery of life I can go over and ride horses with Becky and visit with Les. They have two neat Tennessee Walking horses and this old cowboy still knows how to straddle a saddle just fine!

Whoever has my commands
and obeys them, he is the one
who loves me. He who loves me
will be loved by my Father, and
I, too, will love him and show
myself to him.

John 14:21 (NIV)

Chapter Eleven

IN THE LATE 60s DONNA WANTED to start substitute teaching, which she did, not for the income, but because she missed teaching. Then in 1973 the local superintendent came to her and asked her to take the Liberty Center fourth grade position. We prayed about it and it seemed be a go, so she said yes. Beth was six and in school full time, so there wouldn't be a problem with sitters.

My girl was back in her element!! During the school year the kids and I soon learned that Mom was going to spend at least two hours an evening, and just as likely to spend three, preparing lessons for the next day. We split the chores up among the three of us and then rotated the assignments on a weekly basis so no one got saddled with a nasty set forever.

Our lady loved teaching as much as breathing as far as I am concerned. Keep this comment in mind for recall later on down the road.

Life stayed pretty steady for the next few years, with Doug and Beth and Donna in school and me working mostly six days a week. There were the kids activities and ours as well, a lot of church goings-on, school happenings, and typical family stuff.

Doug was the natural athlete and Beth the scholar. He played baseball in little league and pony league, and played it very well. Now...a dad can brag like that if the numbers are there, and they were! His last year in pony league he batted over 600. That's right, you read right, over 600.

Doug also became quite the runner in junior high and trained to the tune of many miles a week with some really good results in the track meets and cross country. Beth was breezing through her classes during that time and was, to her mom and dad, kind of amazing.

Their social lives were, of course, very busy, and we always were very pleased with the friends they chose. That, dear friends, is a blessing indeed!

Then the first invasion in our health occurred. Well, in Donna's health. She struggled for several weeks with many doctor's visits before they finally informed her she needed a total hysterectomy. She was forty-one years old at the time.

Not too long after that she discovered a prominent lump in one of her hands. On investigation they found a section of veins that looked like a "can of worms." Their terminology, not mine. That resulted in another surgery, a quite painful recovery, and more prayers.

Probably the most uncomfortable surgery she had was a sinus surgery on her left side, but she came through it like a trooper and it seemed to me to more of a bump in the road than expected. But she did suffer a lot of pain afterward.

I failed to realize it at the time, but I now believe Satan was attacking us through her health because of our extremely active engagement in Christian ministry. We were mainly involved as youth advisors at church, but I served on the board, she served on the missions board, and I was involved in the Navigator's 2-7 ministry again.

You might be wondering why I think Satan was directing attacks through Donna rather than straight at me. My answer, and speculation, is this: he saw how deeply we loved each other and figured out that her health problems would halt me much more effectively than my own health problems. I'm a bull-headed get-up-and-swing- again guy and not likely to back off. Unless my love is down, and then I'm going to stop all of life to care for her. That's the plain truth, but it didn't work for him to stop me through her.

God is so wise and so many steps ahead of Satan. He just kept blessing Donna with miracle after miracle along the way so that the result was a woman with one of the deepest faiths and commitments to Jesus of any before or after her.

The result of that was her encouraging me to continue life just as it had been. Now, please understand that I was not and am still not this great spiritual leader at church or at work or anywhere else. I was, and am still, simply vocal about my faith. I'm pretty much happy with life and love to laugh and make people laugh and seldom allowed negative things to hold those traits down. Donna's health was an ongoing negative thing.

But...unless someone was deeply intimate with her like I was, she never appeared down about it. And most of the time, I even had to really be on the ball to detect a down mood.

*Do not be anxious about
anything, but in everything,
by prayer and petition, with
thanksgiving, present your
requests to God. And the peace
of God which transcends all
understanding will guard your
hearts and your minds in Christ
Jesus.*

Philippians 4:6 (NIV)

Chapter Twelve

IN 1978 DOUG AND I JOINED A contemporary Christian band called Shalom, he as a drummer and I as lead guitarist. Doug had really made a science out of drumming and could be heard drumming for hours during the summer up in his room with the windows open to conquer the heat.

We started as a five-piece group and after two years added a young new Christian who was writing a lot of music and needed the affirmation of being in an active Christian group. Donna was an excited supporter of the band, and I know her prayers and those of the others' wives were the answer to any impact we ever had on people's lives.

We were together for four years, disbanding after 1982 because we couldn't find an acceptable keyboard player after the original left for college. That's right, she was a freshman when we started, and could transpose music at the drop of a hat, rewrite on the fly, and was a spectacularly gifted young lady. The fact she had a full ride in college as a cellist said it all.

****

IT WAS THE SPRING OF 1980, DOUG WAS A HIGH school student already, and school was nearly out. Donna needed new glasses because she just could not see very well and was struggling in the classroom. To the optometrist we went. Three different pairs of lenses later, including an attempt to solve the problem with tri-focals, and we were sent to an ophthalmologist in Toledo.

They did a ton of tests and discovered the field vision in her left eye was nil. All she could see out that eye was a tiny speck of light at one place. Now the reason for no success with new lenses had an answer, a nasty one. She was fitted with lenses that brought her right eye up to a 20 x 30 power and we began to watch her adapt to vision in just one eye. All this time there was no complaining, just some sadness and weeping on both our parts.

Here's where my chest begins to really swell out with pride. That girl of ours became just as safe a driver as ever, even though she became quite hesitant to drive in the city. She still taught, she still read, (we were both always voracious readers), and did all the wifely/motherly chores she had always done.

We did vacations together and she saw just as much natural beauty as the other three of us; and later, when it was just her and I, still the same.

Doug graduated high school in '83 and started college at Toledo University, Beth continued school as a top student, and life seemed to settle down after a couple of years.

I had started running in either '72 or '73 and continued to do so, with Donna's blessings. Then in '88 I contacted mono somehow, and even though it was a slight case, my running stopped. Once I recovered from that, the running just didn't seem to come back to me. That was actually to prove to be just fine, because in the spring of '89 Donna's eyes began to once again start going crazy on her.

Back to the ophthalmologist and he struggled with making a diagnosis. Tried this, tried that, determined the problem was something he called low pressure glaucoma and treated her for that with eye drops. Her vision still went downhill.

The guy then determined he should surgically install a relief valve in the right eye to help keep the pressure down, and she had still another surgery. As a result of that surgery she was completely blind for a day with a patch over that eye. I stayed with her and cared for all her personal needs, including feeding her.

Testament to Donna's great personality was her amusement at my telling her a spoon with corn was next and she received mashed potatoes instead. We laughed and giggled for a really long time as we made that meal a wonderful time together. My girl was tough!

The vision continued to deteriorate and the decision was made in the fall to go to the Kellogg Eye Center in Ann Arbor, Michigan for further testing. By then we were so tired physically from all the driving to tests and appointments and we had cried together so much that we began to refer to the summer of '89 as our "summer of sorrows." We both became so horribly tired of fast food that I swore once this was over I would never look another fast food burger in the face. Well, I have partially relented, but still prefer something else.

The Eye Center could find no encouragement for us, and advised her to learn to read Braille while she could still see a little. Then they added an afterthought. They advised us to have a CTC scan, just in case there was something insidious going on inside her head. Later on, as we discussed that after thought, we both claimed it as a blessing from God; yet another of His touches on my girl's life.

We had the CTC scan and received a call from a neurologist the same day. "You have a tumor growing around the optic nerves and the carotid arteries right behind your eyes. You need surgery right away and I want to see you today."

I always had this tendency to drive fast and furious, so we were in Toledo in no time at all. The surgeon was a little Indian guy and showed us what they had discovered. He recommended surgery to remove the tumor that was wrapped around those arteries and optic nerves, then he dropped the bombshell: if he did the surgery there she had a huge percentage of possibility that she would not live through it. However, there were three surgeons he knew of who could do it and, in all likelihood, be successful. I could have hugged that little guy for his honesty.

Then, the tide turned, because a few seconds later I wanted to feed him his desk! Donna's absolute passion for teaching came out strong as she continued to question him as to whether or not and when she would be able to teach after that. He finally shouted at her to "Shut up! You'll never teach again!"

The old Will just about lost control over that, but as I look back, I see he probably did that out of frustration and wanted to get the point across once and for all that there was a whole lot more than teaching involved here.

He named the three different surgeons he recommended and I asked him who he would pick if it was him. He refused to name one above the others, but with some deep questioning we felt the one in Pittsburg was the best choice. The other two were in Ann Arbor and Cincinnati. He kept almost apologizing that one was in Pittsburg which was so far away, but my ire was once again raised because when you're talking about life or death, why in blazes would you worry about the distance!

I now realize, and Donna agreed, that the reason he kept bringing that up was to sort of guide us in that direction. I still believe that. He sent her CTC scan to Pittsburg and the doctor there called us that night!!

This was the week before Christmas in '89. He said we should spend Christmas with the family and then drive to Pittsburg the following day. Wow, this guy was in a hurry. He stressed the importance of quick response, but also said he gave Donna a 95% chance of making it through the surgery okay. He reserved the other 5% because "It is, after all, medicine and we need to remember that." He also said he felt he could preserve a good deal of sight with the procedure. We were excited to hear from him, especially so quickly and with such positive confidence concerning the possible outcome.

Christmas was really different. There was a subdued atmosphere, but Donna and I tried our best to present a positive and faithful attitude for the family. The following day we made the four hour trip to the Presbyterian University Hospital and were directed to their equivalent of a Ronald McDonald house. We secured a room on the third floor, were shown our cabinet and refrigerator space in the basement, and had a good orientation to life in the house. It was as good as any hotel room and only cost us ten dollars a day.

The next day was filled with meeting the surgeon who would be doing the procedure and his head nurse. What a pair of neat people they were, and hopefully still are all these years later. With a bit of probing we learned that he was the top dog for this procedure IN THE WORLD! God had moved in our lives again. The surgeon also traveled the world over teaching the procedure at other facilities.

As we counseled with him, he explained that the FIRST surgery would last fourteen hours, then there would be a week recovery and then a second fourteen hour surgery. Wow. I knew my girl didn't have the stamina to withstand that sort of ordeal without God's mighty intervention and told him so. He was appreciative of our faith.

The next week was spent doing tests and then more testing and then... You get the idea. The place was so huge that guides were assigned to anyone going for any testing. Most of those guides were students at the University of Pittsburg, so we had the occasional monstrous guys who must have been football players. This was at the beginning of the NFL playoffs and I was, at that time, a staunch Browns fan and always vocal about it no matter where I was. (I have since totally rejected the entire NFL because of so many players dishonoring my country by their refusal to honor the National Anthem and the flag during opening ceremonies.)

But...I digress. Being a huge fan, I wore my really dressy Browns sweater during that week while we were being escorted to a test. By escorted, I mean that Donna was in a wheel chair and I tagged along. This escort must have been at least 6'6" and well over 240 pounds with no fat. He was huge! As we walked along the hall, he looked down at me and, I quote, said, "Ya know little man, you're either really brave or really stupid to wear that." I cracked up. He chuckled. (I was relieved at that.)

Donna had tests every day that week and I could almost swear they took her apart and then put her back together. I think they tested the tests! It totally wore her out. When she wasn't having tests, we spent the rest of the days in her room on the ninth floor of the hospital. I stayed with her pretty much all day.

Naturally, when visiting hours were over at 8:00pm, I made my way back to the house and fixed my supper, then watched a little television or visited with the other residents of the house in the basement rec room. I made some lifelong friends there, people we still contact from time to time, especially during the holidays.

There was Kansas, a rodeo champion cowboy and his daughter who were there with her husband who had brain surgery; Bruce, whose wife was also there for that reason, and "Speedy Gonzalez," or just Speedy, as he was a Mexican with his wife in Donna's room whose name Kansas couldn't pronounce so he started the Speedy nickname. Speedy loved it. We spent several coffee breaks a day in the hospital cafeteria for coffee as a foursome and those guys were a real comfort for me, as I know we all were to each other. Trouble with that was I had recently lost nine pounds through really fighting to get them off, and during the three weeks I spent there I put every one of them back on!! I went home weighing 184 pounds again. Drat.

New Years' night, Doctor S. spent a lot of time going over the next day's events. He repeated the two fourteen hour surgeries, what to expect after each one, and what

I, as the hubby, could expect. His message to me was I needn't expect any updates as the day went on because Donna was his patient, not me. He would see me at the end of the fourteen hours, or whenever the surgery was over.

****

JANUARY SECOND, 1990, 6:00 AM. WE WERE IN THE surgery prep room and had spent a lot of prayer time together, plus I had reported everything to the kids and the church, Pettisville Missionary Church, back home and we were both totally relaxed. I'm serious, it was so. We smiled and visited until they said it was time to wheel her away; we said a final short prayer together, and as they wheeled that 110 pound giant of a lady away she had the biggest smile she could ever have and said in a spunky tone, "I'll see you later Honey." I knew she meant it and believed it. So did I, for God had not left us alone from Him for one single moment.

****

I ACTUALLY HAD A LOT OF FUN DURING MY WAIT ON the ninth floor. The first playoff game was on and it was, believe it or not, the Steelers and Browns!! I wore my Browns sweater and had such a good time with the Pittsburg people and nurses. Their reaction to me and my yelling when the Browns scored or made a big play brought big smiles and fake grumpy comments. I could tell we were of one mind; Americans through and through.

Think back about what I told you the doctor said. He predicted two fourteen hour surgeries. At the nine and a half hour point he walked into the waiting room and told me his part was done, and no second surgery would be needed! His associates were closing for him and he needed food and rest.

The total time for the surgery was exactly ELEVEN hours and no further procedure would be needed. God had placed His great hands over the surgeon's and the two together worked a miracle. Now you can understand why I have to write this autobiography; God must be glorified and praised because of the many and great miracles He plastered my little lady with.

Donna was one of those people who reacted to anesthesia as though she had four doses instead of one. She was out for three days, something I expected. I was allowed in once every two hours for ten minutes and simply stood there talking to her for that long. I did something I have never been allowed to forget during that time. All in fun, of course. I saw a sign in the elevator advertising tickets to a University of Pittsburg basketball game with Syracuse.

I called the number, and the guy offered me the tickets AND a ride to the game for next to nothing. I grabbed it and only skipped one time in to see Donna by doing so.

Saw a good game, had a good time, and it was a good break in the action for me. Then the sky fell in that night!

Around three AM my phone rang. Naturally, I was scared out of my wits when I answered. It was the lady at the lobby desk and I feared the worst for Donna. She told me a policeman wanted to see me right away out by my car because someone had noticed the opera window on the driver's side was broken out. You never saw anyone so happy his car was broken into in your life!!

I dressed and went down and had a very interesting time with the cop. He explained that most cars like mine, an '82 Buick Park Avenue, are stolen to just take a joy ride and then they would be ditched. Thing is, during the cold weather Donna had a way of flooding the thing so I had taken a piece of welding rod and bent it into a U shape, pushed it down over the lip of the carburetor so the choke couldn't close all the way forcing Donna to literally pump her little leg off to start it rather than flood it because she always pumped it even when it didn't need it.

The would-be thieves ran the battery down and gave up! The policeman gave me two bits of information that numbed me. First, he gave me a case number for my insurance company and it was in the 700's. This was the fourth of January and that was the number of car thefts or attempted car thefts THAT YEAR! Wow.

Next, he pointed to a high ridge of land with a lot of trees and told me to never go over that ridge or I wouldn't live to come back!! He also said not to walk the streets between the hospital and the house for the same reason. I had enjoyed that walk every night! So much for that walk to tone down the blood pressure.

Things going well didn't stop there. I leafed through the yellow pages and picked a garage nearby, called and arranged for a tow and a repair of the window and the steering column. They had broken the column to bypass the key switch. The guy towed it six blocks, did the window, and gave me an old screwdriver to use instead of

Donna and Mysti during Donna's recuperation.

a key to start it with since he couldn't get the necessary parts in time to actually repair it before I would likely need it to go home. He also charged the battery.

He charged me sixty bucks! There IS an honest man in Pittsburg, Browns fans, and I praise the Lord for him and hope he is still doing a great business after all these years.

****

As Donna started to regain some strength and healing we settled in to see what God had next for us. The days on the ninth floor sort of dragged on, but when they told us we would be going home on a Friday we were shocked! Donna had not gained enough strength for that! However, doctors being who they are and used to having their way, come Friday we bid goodbye to Presby' University Hospital and began a fearful trip home to Liberty Center some four hours away.

I had Donna fixed up in the roomy back seat of the Buick and it went fairly well until she became desperate for a rest stop. I pulled in at the next turnpike plaza and we reluctantly made our way into the building. Could she make it into the restroom on her own? She was weak as a tiny kitten! Well, necessity breeds will power, and away she went. I paced the floor like an expectant father while worrying all the time. Where had my faith gone!?

After several hours, or so it seemed, (it was just a few minutes), she emerged and we were soon on the road again. We finally made it home and she was to be sequestered on the living room pull-out couch for the next few weeks. Her and her little friend, Mysti the family pooch, that is. That little rascal never left her side except to go out to meet her own needs.

The ladies from church then started a help campaign to end all campaigns; the meals began to come on a daily basis and that was a nineteen mile ride one way. Also, a few of them came in during the day so I could return to work. My foreman had bent over backwards and then some to help us with time away, offered to change my hours, and several more things. I stayed on my regular hours since the church gals were doing such wonderful caring for my bride. God's people were teaching us and many others just what this life of serving and helping others is about.

I finally had to call Pastor John and ask him to contact the ladies and ask them to stop bringing food! Our freezer was FULL and we needed to just nuke what was there for great hot meals!

Donna slowly recovered and we had to go back to Pittsburg for a follow-up with the surgeon two weeks later. We dreaded the trip for her, but with the roomy Buick back seat, she made it fine. I seem to remember we stayed two nights and then came home. All of her tests were fine and the prognosis was very positive since the tumor was benign.

She was totally blind in the left eye, and only had sight from the upper left hand quadrant of her right eye. She, therefore, saw more to the left than straight on or right and her peripheral vision had ceased to exist. My life's love was legally blind.

We even stopped for dinner at one of Maumee, Ohio's finest Mexican restaurants on the way home. I guided her in and out in a manner that was to become such habit that I even used it for others when I was walking with them. I still do it sometimes.

Coming to a curb, "You have a down...now." Or, "You have an up...now." The fact that I felt that was necessary guidance never irritated her, nor did we ever consider it strange during the rest of our lives together; it was a new but very real part of our relationship.

It was, however, a bit embarrassing when I would say one of those helps to another guy I was walking with! I did get some strange looks for a while. We even created some special words to make it simpler; "Slown" for a slope down, and, of course, "slup" for a slope up. You should see the looks I got a few times when I forgot who I was walking with!

****

ONCE DONNA WAS COMFORTABLE STAYING ALONE we called off the PMC ladies and began the adaptation process. What a warrior. In a very short time she was cooking, cleaning, and other household chores she had always done before. Yes, she DID rest a bunch more often, and I encouraged her to do so, but within a couple of months she even started reading again.

That first summer we even got adventurous and took the small motorhome we had to New England. Took in the beauty of Massachusetts, Connecticut, and upstate New York and she did quite well considering it had not even been six months yet. God plopped another miracle down on us during that trip. I noticed a problem on the motorhome that required servicing. I "just happened" to see it coming on as we neared an exit and pulled over and off to the side of the exit ramp. We had only been there long enough for me to confirm that it would not be safe to drive when a car stopped and asked if we needed help.

I told the gentleman the problem , said I had tools but required a part. He offered to drive me the "less than half a mile" to the parts store and bring me back. Wow, co-incidence? No way. We were back on the road in less than an hour. Now tell me; just what are the "chances" of breaking down at that spot, in that timing, with the parts needed just a half mile away and transportation available? That, dear ones, was a God thing.

We both loved motorhome travel and did a lot of it. Mostly it was west to the Rockies.

But because of his great love for us, God, who is rich in mercy, made us alive with Christ even when we were dead in transgressions - it is by grace you have been saved.

Ephesians 2:4-5 (NIV)

Chapter Thirteen

DURING THE '90'S I STARTED writing seriously because of an event that triggered my imagination. We were scheduled to go to an event, and no, I don't remember what, but Donna was being the typical wife and not ready when I was. I turned the tube on and there was a western movie just starting. The start of that movie was so exciting that I grabbed a VCR tape and popped it in, hit record, and left it for later. I think it was either a Friday or Saturday evening.

We returned after the event and I went to rewind the tape. Once it was rewound we went to bed and I was ready to watch it Sunday afternoon. Drat, when I started the tape it was something I had recorded and watched before; I had obviously neglected to rewind the tape before hitting record! The start was so dynamic that I was crushed. I can never remember, either before, or since, being so disappointed in not being able to watch a movie. That beginning had me captivated!

The next morning at work I was involved in a job that was simply running conduit and then pulling wire into it for a major installation. Now, just how much brainwork does something as simple as measure, cut, thread, turn into the previous conduit, measure, cut.......you get the picture. So...I decided to make up my own story and add it to the start I had seen.

By the end of the day eight hours later I was hooked! I had a story that was exciting and ready to be written. I decided then and there to write my first novel. I started writing on legal pads, but after thirty pages and having what I had down evaluated by a couple of other people, Donna included, we decided I should purchase a word processor.

We found one made by one of the main typewriter companies that was a word processor and only that. I felt no need for a laptop computer at that time and the cost was about a third of the computer.

I would carry the beast to work and type during my morning break and lunch. By the time those events came around I would have many pages in my thoughts and the three fingers I used to type would just fly. Fly? Well, it was faster than writing, and much easier to read!

Folks ask me how long it took to write a book, but I really don't remember for sure on that first one. The closest I can come to an accurate estimate is eight weeks, but I wrote all the time. The word processor went everywhere I went; to doctor's appointments and was fired up in the waiting rooms; to the hospital during my dad's surgery and then my mom's; to anything that required me to sit for a while. Lonely are The Hunted flowed from my twisted brain like a rushing river and I will never write like that again, even though the sequential stories were a lot of fun to write. I still love it, but, as said before, this particular work is hard to do.

The most rewarding part of writing the first was the way my family upheld me. Donna encouraged me to no end, Beth offered to do my typing, and Doug spent his money on a book with a list of all the literary agents in the US so I could market my book. That still touches me all these many years later; my family believed in me! There was never a doubt in their minds that I could write successfully. How special is THAT?

Once I finished the manuscript I began to submit it to many of the agents listed in the book. Then I began to collect the rejection slips instead of stamps or coins! They all said pretty much the same thing; westerns are dead and no one wants to publish them any more.

That was bunk, because a couple of western writers were being published on a regular basis. I finally gave up and ceased my submissions. I didn't stop writing, though, for I had a second story using the same characters in mind. I had fallen in love with my characters so much that they felt like family!

About six or so chapters in I hit my very first writer's block! My brain went comatose whenever I tried to think about the next part of the story. I decided maybe if I started another story in a totally different genre it might break me loose from the block. That was when I started what is now my fourth published story, Valley of The Shadow. It would not be finished until well into the next century! The genre was a futuristic Christian fiction story based in the year 2023.

My experiment worked, and after six or so chapters in the new one, the western plot came to me as far as continuing and away I went. I worked on the second western until I had about a third of it done and then quit writing, period.

I had a nephew up in Michigan who is a great fan of westerns and somehow he got wind that I had written one and asked to read it. I mailed him a copy right away, not expecting to hear from him on it at all. This was around 2004 or 2005. He called me soon and raved about the story, asking why I hadn't published it.

I explained the rejection stories and figured things would stop there, but he asked if he could have a member of his congregation read it, that the guy was a full time writer. (Tim was a pastor of a church up there.) I said of course he could do that and then forgot about it.

I soon got another call and he requested we go up there so I could meet his friend the writer, because he had a way for me to get published. Well, not one to ignore possibilities, Donna and I did just that. Tim took me to meet Skip, who explained a couple of different ways I could self publish or something I think he called POD, or Print

On Demand. It would require my financing the printing and some other costs. That's what he was doing with his books and he was successful at it.

I declined, explaining my feelings that first, if my writing wasn't worth the cost of publishing to a regular publisher, it wasn't worth the cost to me because all the promotional work would be mine and I just wasn't interested in that. Skip was understanding, but he and I connected as friends at the time. We sort of kept in touch, but not on a regular basis.

Then around the end of 2007 Skip called me to explain that he and his wife, Sara, had been praying for some time about starting a publishing company of their own in order to better publish his books. They had done that and were experiencing some success with it. Now they felt God would have them publish other authors and he told me they would like publish "my cowboy story."

I consented, and *Lonely Are The Hunted* became a real, honest to goodness book published by White Feather Press in 2008 with Skip and Sara Coryell at the helm. Skip somehow got wind that I was working on a sequel and insisted on also publishing it and the next thing I knew, I had a contract for three westerns!

As a result, The Rocky Mountain Odyssey series containing three westerns became a reality. The second book is *Rocky Mountain Odyssey* and number three is *Shadow of Vengeance*. The other work? I finally felt I should finish it and did so and now *Valley of The Shadow* is a reality in the Christian fiction genre. They haven't made me rich, but I wouldn't trade the experience for anything. To have people like White Feather Press put their trust in my work, and to see some exciting sales at times has been a real blessing.

I really get a thrill out of reader response, also. The most amusing response was a letter from a man who asked me, "How do you think you know what a woman would think in many cases? We men don't think like them, so what makes you think you can write about them?"

My response was simple and succinct: "I'll soon be married fifty years and we talk to each other. I think I'm very qualified because I have a great teacher."

Now...think about the circumstances that occurred to bring Skip and me together. The timing involved, the contact with a nephew I hadn't seen for years, all those things that happened at "just the right time" to trigger Skip's interest in my work. You cannot convince me that God did not bring those things about in just the right timing, HIS timing.

LONELY

ARE THE

HUNTED

Will Riley Hinton

Book one in the Rocky Mountain
Odyssey adventure series

For since the creation of the world God's invisible qualities - his eternal power and divine nature - have been clearly seen, being understood from what has been made, so that men are without excuse.

Romans 1:20 (NIV)

Chapter Fourteen

WISH I COULD REMEMBER THE FIRST year we traveled west to the Rockies. It was while Donna could still drive, so it was before 1989; and it was while we were attending Pettisville Missionary Church so it had to be between 1985 and '89.

We had the most wonderful time together. We took our two room tent and camped a lot while in the mountains, but did the motel thing while on the way out and back. We spent three days with her brother and family in Phoenix then went north to the Grand Canyon, camping over night there. We arrived after dark, pitched the tent, and retired for the night as soon as we had supper over with. We were whipped.

The next morning I arose and went out through a little copse of twisted, gnarled trees, stepping into the clear about ten feet from the rim. I stood glued to the spot, tears running down my cheeks at the unbelievable sight of what God had wrought there. I sensed a presence at my elbow and glanced down to see this very pretty lady standing next to me, tears also flowing freely from her eyes. We shared that moment that drew us closer than ever because of His presence with us.

Don't ever let anyone tell you being married doesn't multiply your prayer power by more than twice; it is some huge power of ten because of the scripture that says "Where two or three agree on anything, it shall be done." You become one in marriage, yes, but that one still combines two hearts into a power way too many couples fail to trust.

Camping via motor home was
a huge part of our lives.

That trip was so spectacular that as we motored along on our way to Rocky Mountain National Park, on the ninth day, Donna said, "You know, Hon, I've run out of superlatives. I feel saturated and sort of approaching numb."

I replied that I, too, was pretty much done in as far as really being aware of new sites. We decided to camp that night and then head for Ohio early. It wasn't because of any disappointment, it was just the opposite; it was almost like too much ice cream!

A work mission in Jamaica.

The next trip was in our second motor home with her older brother, Denny, and his wife Betty . We had a really wonderful trip, and that kicked off many more. We were hooked on "my" Rockies!

There was a moment after I had retired that I was working on one of the westerns when Donna asked me how it was going. I told her I was sort of out of energy for it at that time and her next question was, "Should we pack?" She felt a trip west would inspire me again, and she was right. We took off shortly after that and had a blast with just the two of us. When we got back, I started back on *Odyssey* and finished it soon after.

We often claimed to qualify as tour guides for Colorado and Wyoming, but those wonderful states are so vast and gorgeous that those being guided would wonder about their guides just standing, mouths open, eyes stretched wide and hearts beating a hundred miles an hour. Those were our typical responses, even in places where we had visited many times. For God to love mankind enough to give us sights like those to enjoy and marvel at is more testament of His great care. Wow.

*Therefore go and make disciples
of all nations, baptizing them in
the name of the Father and of
the Son and of the Holy Spirit,
and teaching them to obey
everything I have commanded
you. And surely I am with you
always, to the very end of the
age.*

Matthew 28:19-20 (NIV)

Chapter Fifteen

SHOULD TITLE THIS CHAPTER. IT would be: Missionary work missions.

We had the great privilege of going on several work missions during our time together, and each was a life changing-journey. Our first was with folks from the Liberty Chapel EUB and we were able to take Beth and a friend with us. My memory isn't being kind to me here as to how many went, but it was somewhere around ten or twelve. We traveled to Wedowee, Alabama to help out at a Christian camp there that brought missions people in from foreign countries and taught them ways to improve the lifestyle in the field.

Before you get the wrong idea, a good example of this was teaching people from the high mountains of Peru how to make solar ovens in order to be able to stop burning dried dung to cook with. The fumes from the burning dung were found to be responsible for ruining the eyesight of many of the women in their villages, so this was a way out of that.

They also taught people how to make gravity water pumps to pump water uphill from streams to the villages. There were many ways they helped the students to cope with natural problems. Our jobs varied while we were there, and a brother Dennis and I wired the new cafeteria/class room building.

The place was a lovely mountain area with a gorgeous mountain stream running right through it. We availed ourselves of that stream every single day after work! Talk about coooold. I loved to sit downstream from one of the little waterfalls with my back against the rock where the water flowed over and just let it try to drown me.

The campsite was about a quarter mile from the buildings, and Donna and I put our tent up and let the girls have that while we set up our cots in the bathroom building! It was cooler, and quieter. I know that sounds unreal, but we got along just fine! We slept in a space between the two restrooms and the sinks and felt like we had the best of it.

I was spared an injury by a miracle during the trip. I had checked power to a light I was hooking up. It was dead, and instead of going to the breaker panel and securing the appropriate breaker, I just went ahead and wired the beast. During that time I handled both wires at the same time while feeding them into the fixture, and a couple of other times as well.

I got the fixture hooked up, assembled the reflector, put the fluorescent tubes in and was greeted by a lot of light! They came on! The circuit was hot.

I rushed to the breaker panel to find someone had flipped that circuit on for one reason or another. Since I was working near the top of a ten foot stepladder, I would have experienced an injury of some type had not God intervened. That was not to be the last miracle while there.

Three of the local volunteers helping were elementary teachers, all men. Each evening after showers, supper, and the cold stream, we sat around in the new cafeteria playing Trivial Pursuit with them and others. They were really neat guys and Donna and I became very close to them. I chuckled at some of the hard discussions she triggered about phonics and how did they possibly teach children to talk like they did using incorrect phonics? It got really funny sometimes between the four of them, but I "helped" keep the peace. (Yeah, right.) (NOT.)

Each night once the "party" broke up, Donna, three or four others and I walked back the quarter mile to the camp area and tucked ourselves in. It was always a pleasant walk in the dark, warm night and was the final relaxing time for that day.

On the last night before we were to leave the three local guys had parked up at the camp ground just so they could walk with us for that last time. As we prepared to lock the door to the cafeteria one of the guys asked who had the light. We told him we didn't need or use a light and all three had the blood drain from their faces! "You haven't walked up there in the dark?"

I teased and assured them Ohioans aren't afraid of the dark. One asked, "How about rattlesnakes, you afraid of them?" It was very quiet for a bit until another of them told us, "The snakes crawl out onto the blacktop roads at night to soak up the heat. You mean no one has stepped on a snake all week?"

THAT took the wind out of our sails, I'll tell you! We searched around until we found a flashlight and walked in a close huddle all the way to the camp! After a lot of hugs and some tears we said goodnight to our friends and turned in. We never forgot that week for many reasons, but that fact that Donna and I felt the Lord had prevented any encounters with snakes was mentioned for many years. We embraced that as yet another miracle from Him.

****

OUR NEXT MISSION TRIP WAS IN LATE JANUARY AND early February of 2000 to Jamaica. The church sent a team of men and women down to build a new administration building for a church camp called Kendall Camp. It was high on a beautiful hill that many called a mountain, but with my southeastern Ohio background, it is a hill.

We had great accommodations as the main building was structured like a motel with two stories of individual rooms complete with bathrooms. After the two hour very bumpy ride from the airport, the beds were a welcome respite!

We settled into a routine that consisted of those gals assigned to kitchen duty arising around 5:00 am to prepare breakfast for the rest of us. Since that was Donna's assignment, I got up with her and walked the grounds in the dark with my portable CD player giving me contemporary Christian music as I prayed and worshipped in that beautiful "darkest hour" setting. Each morning I ended up just outside the kitchen window on a neat little alcove facing the east so that I saw the sun rise every morning as it arrived in the notch between two real mountains to our east. It reminded me of a target in a gun sight and was breathtaking each time. Those were wonderful mornings for me and the Savior spoke to me many times through the music and through my heart. The trip was worth it all just for those morning experiences with Him.

Still Jamaica, clowning around
at the end of the day.

The team built the new structure using cement blocks, and our buddy Jim mixed all the mortar and concrete by hand that was used during those two weeks. He was an animal and there were times when Brian and I thought he would literally kill us with work! I also ran all the necessary electrical conduit for the wiring during the time there.

Near the end of the second week we were pouring cement down into the openings of all the blocks in the walls, a requirement there because of the hurricanes they had from time to time. You never saw so much rebar and such on one building here in the states! I was up on a scaffold carrying five gallon buckets of cement to pour into the wall when the board on which I was walking broke with the weight. Having the heavy bucket of cement in my right hand it jerked me to a horizontal position and I was falling on my way to the ground about seven feet below when I hit my back on the scaffold, which turned me back to a vertical position with big Jim grabbing me to stabilize me as I landed, feet first, and never went down.

The bucket didn't even spill, as far as I know! My back was a mess from the abrasions caused by the scaffold poles, but what's a little blood compared to a broken arm or two?! I was blessed once again by the Lord's caring and looking after me! The most negative part of it was that the crew leader, who never cared much for me, blamed the accident on my being careless! That brought the old pre-Christian Will out and I was about ready to feed him the broken plank. (Calm down, ya old hillbilly, just calm down.)

We achieved a tremendous amount of work on the building and had the walls up, filled, and ready for roof AND floor. They would pour the cement floor during the next work team's two weeks.

Both Donna and I grew during that time, and it was a huge blessing for us both. The only negative thing other than my accident and attitude after it was that Donna discovered many years later that I had deliberately lied to her about there not being any chameleons on the walls in our room. Others had talked about them the whole two weeks and I knew Donna would never sleep if she thought there were any lizards with us, so I told her repeatedly there were no chameleons in our room at any time. Well, there was only ONE, after all, and he wasn't all that big.

****

OUR NEXT THREE MISSION TRIPS WERE TO WARREN-ton, Missouri, to work at Child Evangelism Fellowship. If you remember Donna's internship for missions, I mentioned that she had taught classes for CEF while there. Those classes convinced her CEF was one of the top evangelistic arms in the US. While there it was amusing to all of us that Donna drew duty GRADING PAPERS for the students who were taking courses by mail. (It is called "The Mailbox Club") That girl was in her element! She loved it.

We rode down with two of our best friends from PMC, and their cousin was in the carload behind us plus several others. I think we took three carloads if I remember right. Willie did landscaping and garden work, I don't remember what many of the others did, but I drew electrical work. (Imagine that.) Had a great week the first time down and made some new friends for life. One was Marvin, the guy in charge of the Mailbox Club who was also a cousin to Willie and Elaine. Marv is a bass player and organized a jam session one evening in the middle of the week and we played 'til the wee hours. Had a good bunch of musicians and raised the roof. I had taken one of my guitars and an amp because Willie and Elaine had threatened me with violence if I failed to do so.. Okay, maybe not, but they did strongly suggest it. I was glad I did.

The following trip was much the same a year later, then we went for a two week trip the third year. Each time was a huge blessing for us, and, I think, for all who went. We saw God at work first hand.

I maintain and strongly believe you cannot go on any trip of that type and come back unchanged because God never fails to show up. Drop everything right now and go find one for you! Okay, maybe later, but I am only partly in fun with that comment. Mission trips, whether stateside or foreign will draw you closer to God the Father and Christ the Son as well as the Holy Spirit. I guarantee you it WILL change you as a Christian.

He saved us, not because of
righteous things we had done,
but because of His mercy.. He
saved us through the washing of
rebirth and renewal by the Holy
Spirit.

Titus 3:5 (NIV)

Chapter Sixteen

ONCE WE WERE BACK INTO something of a routine after the brain surgery and Donna began to recuperate she started walking a lot. She really didn't have another choice open to her with the fact she was now legally blind. It was half a mile from the house on Maple street to the grocery uptown, and other than that there wasn't anything else to draw her out.

Oh, yes, we had a great hardware, a bank, and a library, but how many of those did she ever use? As a result we talked things over and decided it was time to downsize, and with that action, to possibly get her to a place where she could reach other stores and services. We started looking for a different place, a smaller place.

During our search we even contemplated buying a lot and putting up a modular home, and as we considered that we traveled into the modular home industry center just over the Indiana line, That was interesting, and we had pretty much settled on a design when our realtor called and said she had found our new place.

We met with her at the proposed place on Stevenson Street in Napoleon and fell in love. It was a small, two bedroom home of 1150 square feet, the perfect size for us. There was a two and a half car garage with an additional 14 X 18 foot shop on the back, plus a full basement. I stepped into the empty 20 X 24 foot back room of the basement and, in spite of there being only two 60 watt bulbs glowing there, I saw in my mind a fantastic shop!

Donna saw a good living space with nice kitchen, living room, and all the good things a happy couple could use. It was also a five minute walk from a grocery store, salon, barber, and a ten minute walk from downtown Napoleon in the other direction. Bam...we bought it.

We moved the weekend before Thanksgiving in 1996 with a lot of help from our church friends and family. The little house was right beside a creek running through town and that was a nice addition to the surroundings; it was around twelve feet to the bottom and heavily lined with trees. The water typically ran around a foot deep, but really moved a lot of water during storms.

The backyard was a nirvana for me! The back patio was around four to five feet higher than the lawn behind it, settled among some huge maple trees and I loved to sit out there and read, write, play guitar, or just gawk at the birds and squirrels. One of my all-time favorite spots ever.

A very big plus for me was the drive to work being cut from nine miles to two. BUT! That really became a negative because those nine miles from Liberty were my every day prayer time and I cherished that time. It wove a protection around my day, and it afforded me an uninterrupted time alone with Jesus. I shamefully admit that my amount of time spent in prayer became frustratingly scattered, or fragmented.

Yes, that was my own fault, and I corrected it from time to time, but I still missed that nine miles. Now, the winter driving was much more pleasant for sure, and there were very few times I was snowed or iced out of work.

Our lives took on a wonderfully quiet existence and we both thoroughly enjoyed each other. In 1998, when I was fifty-eight, Campbell's offered a buy-out and I was set to take it and move to another job I had been offered. When I mentioned it, I got the old "deer-in-the-headlights" look from my sweet lady. I knew immediately she was frightened of the prospect, so I relented and bypassed the opportunity.

Two years later she came to me and said, "I've been looking at our finances, and if we draw from the 401K for a couple of years I think you could get out of there." HA! I turned my notice of retirement in the next day. So on June 30th, 2000 I escaped from the factory and we entered into a period of life that drew us closer every single day as we were free to plan whatever and whenever we desired.

I did some volunteer electrical work for some people, really immersed myself in model airplane competition, and in 2001, I answered the call of my heart to build my dream electric guitar. I gathered together some used parts, a little special wood, and went for it.

I had sold my Gibson Les Paul, purchased new when I was eighteen in 1958, and used half the cash to buy a used Paul Reed Smith. I had never heard of the brand, having dropped out of the music scene for many years. I'll say it here, that is the Stradivarius of manufactured electric guitars, at least in my opinion. I started playing it a little bit in the basement, then went out to my buddy Larry's for a jam session and came home a different guitarist. That thing played like butter and got me back into playing, it was so incredible.

Being me, I couldn't justify having a four thousand dollar guitar that wasn't being used in my possession, so I swapped it off. However, when I decided to build a guitar, I promised myself if I couldn't make it play like the PRS, I'd hack it up!

With some internet study and a lot of perseverance I had what I wanted, took it to church and sent it home with three different players. All of them raved about the way it played. That's when Donna made the big mistake...she said I should build those for other people! A light bulb over my head came on! That's a go, little lady.

In 2001 I started doing just that, developed four different models of solid body electric guitars and started taking them to guitar shows. Donna and I had a blast meeting tons of people at those, and I even sold a few. At a show in Columbus, Ohio I was approached by a fellow who was opening a new music store and he wanted five instruments, one for his own and four to have in the store.

We worked out a deal and I went home higher than the proverbial kite.

I spent a lot of time in the shop building the instruments he wanted, had them done in a little under two months and delivered them to Columbus. It made a nice day trip for us and while there we met with Steve and his wife for dinner besides visiting his store. I would make several trips down during the next few months and was disappointed when they decided to move to California. There went my retail outlet. Oh well, life goes on.

After a couple of years of going to the guitar shows and really loving it, we talked it over and decided since it was costing more than we were making from them we should just skip that part of the deal. In a way that was a bummer because we had never enjoyed any joint venture more. We got to meet tons of nice folks and witness to many about our Lord.

Just a little bit about that last statement; I chose "Crossover Custom Guitars" for my brand name and that was on every tuning head I turned out, and has been on every one of the forty-some instruments to date. Along with that nomenclature is the scripture reference John 5:24 in hopes they will look it up. My reason for those choices is this: in the NIV, John 5:24 says, (and these are the words of Jesus) "I tell you the truth, anyone who hears my words and believes on the One who sent me has everlasting life and will never come in to condemnation but has CROSSED OVER from death to life."

See where my Crossover brand comes from?

Things have not always been smooth for the guitar business. The state of Ohio Taxation Department lost my sales tax return three different times. I had to trek to Toledo to their office with my paperwork and cancelled check to get it all worked out. I was successful twice, but the third time was after I had had a-fib problems and did no business for the final six months of the previous year. Hence, no cancelled check.

I did have my copy of the return, however, but they refused to allow it because they claimed I could have just made it out at that time in order to avoid being fined. I was as hot as I've ever been. I cancelled my vender's license right then and there.

Since then I have stayed in the same "business" as before, but I don't charge anything for my services. People pay for their parts and nothing more. You see, I had long since discovered that I felt God would have me be a service for Christian musicians as a ministry, not a business, and had already started working that way.

My comment is this when folks complain that I am worth their paying for my time. "My time belongs to Him, so pay Him whatever you think it's worth." I am kept wonderfully busy as a luthier doing many repairs and setups as well as building many instruments. I am, at this date in July of 2018, building my forty-sixth and forty-seventh guitars/basses. If you do the math on those numbers, I have averaged about two and three quarters instruments a year as far as building. I'm quite happy with those numbers.

During the summer, (spell that "flying season") I'm a lot slower than winter time, except for the holidays, and they slow me down for family events. Hey, this old hillbilly tries to keep his priorities straight!

All in all, God has so completely blessed me in this that I tell people I am living the dream. More on that later, as I tell you about my new workshop.

I still play a little lead guitar at church on occasion, and pick a little in the basement, but my playing has really diminished in comparison to a long time back. I often miss the weekly jam sessions I used to participate in, but time has turned me in different directions. I have been asked the question, "How long will you continue building and fixing them?"

My answer is always the same: "As long as I can still breath and stand." I will also continue playing until these old arthritic hands say "No more!" That hasn't happened yet, in fact; even with having to slow down on the neck I feel I'm a much better guitarist for that reason. I once told a young friend after a church service he needed to use "fewer notes, more feeling." I stand by that and like what I play.

*Therefore, I urge you, brothers,
in view of God's mercy, to offer
your bodies as living sacrifices,
holy and pleasing to God - this
is your spiritual act of worship.*

Romans 12:1 (NIV)

Chapter Seventeen

I THINK I NEED TO TOUCH ON THE model airplane part of life in a bit more detailed manner because of some of the "God sightings" present there. When I started flying "real" airplanes and was called by God to establish the missionary flying service my modeling hobby had to cease; there was just no time left.

When I lost my medical certificate in 1978 as a result of my, shall we say, stupidity, all flying activities were now history. Watching my two offspring finish school, play sports, do the typical teenage growing up activities took all my attention. Don't get that statement wrong, it was a very rewarding and exciting time. Our children never embarrassed us and we were proud parents. Oh, sure, there were issues, but none so terrible they couldn't be solved peacefully.

Just before Donna's second eye started to give problems I got the desire to start modeling again and built a new "stunt" ship, a copy of one I had designed in the late 60s. The term "stunt ship" is really called a precision aerobatics model and is used to fly a precision aerobatics program consisting of fifteen maneuvers on two control lines so all the maneuvers are contained in a hemisphere. It is considered by many to be one of the more difficult events one can fly with a model airplane.

It was/is absolutely my favorite event. The models used are very beautiful and must be built by the competitor flying them. I contacted a man I knew of who provided

My own design for competition; it served me well.

special wings made of foam and asked him some questions about the process of making them because that was the route I planned to take.

He was the chief editor of Flying Models (FM) magazine, a world wide publication. As I told him the ship I planned to build and that it would be my second one he got quite excited and was interested in publishing it as a construction article in FM! I was stoked! That had been something of a dream of mine ever since I had been building models.

We made contact many times during the following months to work out details on the article. One day during a call I had made during my lunch I said it was time for me to return to work and he stopped me. He said, "Will, we've talked about several of the fliers both of us knew when you were flying stunt the previous years, but there's one person I think we both know from things you have said that we haven't mentioned or talked about."

I asked him who he meant and he said, "The man from Galilee." We witnessed of a faith in Christ right there and then, and he made another comment that would change my life again. He said, "We need a Christian organization for stunt flyers."

I challenged him to start one but he explained that he was just way too busy to even think about it and the conversation ended there with a congenial goodbye.

I had entered the national championships for 1990 with every intention of finally getting to attend my very first nationals. It had been a dream of mine since childhood to just attend, let alone compete. Then Donna's trials came along and I decided I didn't need to go, in fact, shouldn't go because of her being in a recovery mode.

The "nats" were to be during the early weeks of July and her surgery was on January second of that year so I planned to stick with her. She had a fit. Well...not quite THAT bad, but insisted she could manage for a week

This ship was my favorite.
I flew it for several years.

without me. By the time July came around my kids had convinced me they would be there for Mom and I should go; that I needed the time for myself. (Told you I had good kids.)

I had a control handle failure the week before the nats and lost the airplane to terra firma; you know; ball diamond one, Will nothing. Since I already had a room reserved and all the plans in place I decided to go anyway if only to observe. There were a few people planning to see me there whom I had always wanted to meet and who had expressed the desire to meet with me.

The nats in 1990 were held in Lawrenceville, Illinois, and I stayed in a hotel in Vincennes, Indiana where most of the precision aerobatics competitors were staying. There were close to a hundred entries that year in the two classes and I planned on enjoying my first experiences, plane or no plane.

My first day there was the day before competition was to start and I attended appearance judging for the first time, a true treat to see all those beautiful models. Then I drove out to the airport where the competition was being flown to watch practice flights and meet a few of the guys I was looking forward to seeing.

My article had been published and was out a week prior to that, I had even received a letter from a fellow in California commenting on the article and the plane, both quite complimentary. He gleaned from some things I had written that we just might be brothers in Christ and recommended I meet with a friend of his named Gid who was also a dedicated Christian and very good flier.

God stepped in, of course, and I met Gid when I heard him say he had to get back to the hotel and try to find a roomie to share the expenses with. He had been pointed out to me previously, so I knew who he was and quickly collared him! We ended up rooming together, and in the process I agreed to be his mechanic for the week to hold his plane while starting it and then launching it for him.

Gid also ask me to watch his pattern and do any coaching I thought he needed. I knew the pattern then and still know now what works and what scores high, so I agreed to do that. We established a really good friendship, and as I saw him get up in the morning and read his Bible and pray I knew he had a heart for Jesus.

God had been nudging me toward that Christian organization thing my friend and publisher Bob had brought up and as I put the idea in front of Gid, he got really excited. By the time the week was out, I knew the Lord was calling on me to establish yet another Christian organization.

Gid finished fourth in the championships and was ecstatic with those results. So was I, and the week was a true success for me because I now knew a ton of well known fliers with whom I could associate for witnessing.

However, I really was homesick for Donna before the week was out! I couldn't wait to get home and was on the road at four am the last day. As soon as we settled down when I got home I told her about the call I was feeling from God and she just smiled and nodded. I knew I had her backing.

We started taking the motor home to area contests and I would put out a sign advertising a morning devotional for Sunday morning before competition started. We might have two other people, sometimes as high as five, and I also sort of advertised in the newsletter for PAMPA, the Precision Aerobatics Pilot's Association.

I got a few responses, and one football coach from North Carolina went so far as to suggest the name of Fellowship of Christian Modelers for the group, patterned after the Fellowship of Christian Athletes. Sounded good to me, so I went with that.

In 1993 the governing body of all model competition, the Academy of Model Aeronautics, (AMA), had a homecoming at the newly purchased and developed national headquarters site just outside of Muncie, Indiana on a two square mile property. It was to host all the disciplines of modeling and was to be entertainment only, no competition. Donna and I took the motor home and parked at the control line site for the weekend. Control line is what I fly where there are two braided stainless steel lines going out to the airplane that control the up and down movement of the plane. They can be anywhere from twenty to sixty-five feet long, depending on the size and power of the plane. (I typically fly the maximum length of 65 feet.)

On the first full day, Saturday, I met a young fellow still in high school who I helped with a problem he had on his plane. I then invited him to the camper for a break and presented the gospel to him. He shared that he already had faith in Christ and so I shared the vision of FCM with him.

He got really excited over that and dragged me out to meet Allen Goff, another forward speaking brother. (You probably have noticed that I share only first names in here until now just in case someone might object to having their name out there. I use Allen's full name because I know, first, he won't object and second, the organization I'm about to tell you about would not thrive without his energy and devotion.)

When Allen and I met, we clicked instantly. You could use the term love at first sight and it would be accurate. When he came to our camper he and Donna also clicked right away. I shared the concept of FCM with him and it was practically a done deal right then and there.

We started promoting things but the Lord wasn't ready yet for us to really latch onto the concept until 1995. Allen and a buddy plus Donna and I attended a big weekend at Sig Manufacturing in Montezuma, Iowa that year. It was an annual event organized by the model manufacturer and was huge in scope. The weekend was always well attended and a lot of fun.

Allen and I met some other Christians that weekend and shared the vision with everyone we could. We asked for permission to hold a worship service on Sunday morning early, got the approval, and started advertising.

Sunday morning we had somewhere in the mid to high twenties in attendance and left that morning with our first board of directors! There were six of us committed to furthering the concept.

One of those was an airline pilot from the Chicago area who asked a lawyer friend to help us procure our 501(c)3 status with the IRS. Within a few weeks we were officially a designated non-profit organization and God took over from there. I was president and Allen became our national director. His became the key office in the organization and he remains in that capacity yet today. He does a tremendous job of promoting FCM, organizing things, and just being mister jack of all trades for us.

There became a misconception in the ranks that FCM was strictly a control line organization and that was hard to overcome for a while. Then a major hobby supplier/ manufacturer entered in and paid for a quarter page ad for us in Model Aviation, the key publication of the AMA. Things changed.

God has now taken us to a membership of somewhere in the vicinity of 1500 members in the USA and with members in thirteen foreign countries. Don't get me wrong, some of those countries have only one or two members.

We have an international prayer chain run by email, which I now care for, and a monthly newsletter called The Crosswinds that goes out via email. (Guess who publishes THAT?) Yup, you got him. Mister do it all. I hope he never runs down!

****

I COMPETED AT THE NATS FROM THE EARLY 90s UN-til around 2012 when I just got tired of flying alone at home. No one within miles flew the same event I did; most everybody flew radio control. During those years I also made as many smaller contests as I could and was on the verge of qualifying for expert class when I stopped practicing.

To compete at the nats required being there at the AMA site for a week. I stayed at Allen's house with a couple other guys during that week and had a real blast. I didn't really do much as far as high placing in the advanced class until my last year, but it was sooooo rewarding just to be there in the mix and fellowship with people you didn't see but a couple of times a year.

When we moved from the house in Liberty Center to the little place in Napoleon I went to the nats in '97. When I got back on a Saturday and we were hugging it out in the hallway, I asked the normal question, "How was your week?" Of course, we had talked by phone at least twice a day all week, so I was surprised when she said it wasn't a very good week. When I asked her why she said she had felt really down and sad all week, and for no good reason.

My reaction was instantaneous and was prompted by the Holy Spirit. I immediately prayed and claimed victory over Satan and cast him and all his warriors out in Jesus' name. Donna got this incredible look on her face and about jumped up and down. She said she felt an instant release and a joy came on her.

The main reason the Holy Spirit was able to get my attention so quickly was this: of the two of us, Donna and I, SHE was by far the stronger Christian. That girl lived and breathed Jesus. During those fifty-one years together I watched her just never stop growing in her faith. I boldly proclaim now that no one - not Peter, not James, not John, ever loved Jesus MORE than Donna did. It's simply the fact.

So...if she was depressed during that week, she just HAD to be under attack! We both learned a lesson that day, but failed to carry it out for the next nats. When I came home in '98 the same thing had happened. We made our stand against Satan again, the load lifted again.

Just before I left for the next year's time I got some olive oil and went to every possible opening on the house and anointed the tops of those in the name of Jesus with that oil, proclaiming no entry could be had by any of our spiritual enemies. When I got home that time, Donna said she had the absolute best week ever! That continued to happen year after year, and in fact, Donna began to tell me she got so much more done in the house while I was gone and had just a wonderful time with the Lord. Satan is real, dear friends, and he hates us. Ha! JESUS is also real, and He has all ready conquered Satan, so claim that power from HIM!

I still have that ingrained love for model airplanes and precision aerobatics. I might start flying again some day, I'll always have the urge to build; but for right now, 2018, my building is concentrated on custom guitars for people to use to worship Him. I don't want you to think that is a grandiose statement meant to draw praise, it's just who He has shown me He wants me to be for right now. (And I am enjoying it to the fullest.) I tell folks I am living the dream, and I mean it.

I have a lot of balsa wood in my supply cabinet, lots of parts on hand, many world class engines, and I can whip up a competitive stunt ship any time I want, so I'm sure that part of my life isn't done for, just on hold for now. But I still am completely involved with FCM. I resigned from president, but retained the treasurer's position and run the internet international prayer chain via email.

At the time of this writing the guitar building and re-pair has taken over my time, and I'm in the mood for that to be my main time consumer. I am sure the airplanes will once again invade my life in the future, they always do, but for now I am simply a judge and observer.

I tell you the truth, whoever hears my word and believes him who sent me has eternal life and will not be condemned; he has crossed over from death to life.

John 5:24 (NIV)

Chapter Eighteen

AFTER DONNA HAD REGAINED most of her strength in the early 90s, and we had settled into a fairly calm and almost normal existence, we sat back to look at our lives and try to figure out what might be next for us.

Beth had three fine boys, Doug had two, and all was going pretty well. When Beth needed a little help with babysitting, Donna decided to go a couple of times a week to do just that. I would drop her off at Beth's on my way to work and stop for her at the end of the day. I went to work at 6:30 am, so Donna was up really early. She did that for a really long time and had a wonderful influence on the "boys."

Beth was working her corporate job successfully while Doug was teaching fifth grade at Liberty Center, and life just sort of drifted along in a fairly smooth fashion. We had settled in to a life no one would have thought unusual.

I have already chronicled the move and such, but there is an incident that happened in my personal life that I simply must tell about. Donna, being the helps person she was decided to walk over to Beth's house, a mere ten minutes away, and clean house for her. She took off with her smile glowing and as I watched her go, it really warmed my heart. There was a legally blind lady walking off to clean house for someone else and her own kitchen was piled with the morning and lunch-time dishes. What a lover.

I decided if Donna could give up her own chores to do another person's, I could do hers as a reward. (I am NOT a kitchen chores kind of guy.) I put a Phil Keaggy CD in, hit play, and went to work on the dishes.

Phil has one particular song with a line that says, "Go, go all you burdens, go fly away" and when that line came out the Holy Spirit hit me and hit me hard. There were physical hot and cold ripples of current that ran from the top of my head to my toenails and I found myself on my knees without knowing it was happening. I don't have any idea how long I was down there, but when I quit praying and thought things through, I knew this was what happened.

For whatever reason, at that time, God spoke both spiritually and physically to me and He didn't do it to show me sin in my life, He didn't do it to show me a new calling for my life, He had no other purpose but to tell me, in a most spectacular way, that He loves me!!

I have reviewed that moment many, many times and can come to no other conclusion. How wonderful is THAT?! I cannot explain why He has chosen to reveal Himself to me in the manners and many times He has done it, but there is no doubt in my mind about the reality of those times. They have been too spectacular. Remember, they have not ALWAYS been good messages! Remember my MG.

Thoughts come to my mind at times like this when I'm recalling life with Donna and our Lord together. The many, many times she would smile at me and say, "The Lord and I had a wonderful time together this morning." She would then go on and explain some of the things they experienced together during devotions, or on the back patio, or over the kitchen sink. Yep, I said "over the kitchen sink." God can and does show up just about everywhere if you look for Him and seek Him. That's what it takes. Donna knew that, practiced that, and lived for that.

We really enjoyed watching our kids and grandkids grow up, then enjoying their choices of how to make a living. How interesting it has been to see those choices made and then followed through with. Donna was especially blessed by Lincoln, Beth's youngest, because he would visit with her during the summer several days a week and they would play monopoly together. I was still working during those days, so it was wonderful for her to have company during the day.

Of course, with Donna, she did just fine when alone, because she really wasn't alone. Plus, she had those wonderful things we call "books." The question just slipped up on me right now; I wonder just how many books she and I have read during our lives?

And...do we count those we've read more than once? I'm guilty of that more than she was, but nevertheless, that swells the number considerably. Shoot, I've even read those that I WROTE MYSELF more than once. Hey, it helps me evaluate my writing to do that, so no apology here.

****

WE MADE TRIPS TO MY OLD HOME AREA OFTEN TO see my folks. Donna loved them as much as I did and delighted in visiting them in spite of the five hour drive. Remember, the airplane was gone so the hour flight wasn't available any more. (Blast my hide!)

On one trip down I had been shopping for a Honda something for a second car for work, and we decided to stop at a Honda dealer on the east side of Columbus since we went right by it on the six lane. I told the salesman what I needed and about needing the room for a sixty inch span airplane so I could haul it to contests in the more frugal car.

They had nothing in the line of the Civic that qualified both in that part and price. We walked by a little Honda CRX, a sports car look if I ever saw one, and I asked the guy to lift the hatchback. Then I asked him if he had a tape measure and he was off like a shot to borrow one from a mechanic. I checked that little gem out from stem to stern and determined a stunt ship would fit.

It only had 42,000 miles on it and was reasonably priced, but I made a low ball offer. The guy went into his boss and explained where we were from and my offer, then came out with a counter offer.

"Too high, " was my reply and made a counter, still very low. When the salesman came back out he told me his boss was bound and determined to sell a Honda to someone in the Toledo area no matter what! I bought that thing for a song. We had it for ten years, and I might still be driving it if I hadn't missed seeing a hidden water hose underneath everything when I replaced all the other hoses and belts at the hundred thousand mile mark. That fun little car ran like a scared rabbit and still gave me at least thirty-eight MPG on every tank.

****

LET ME RECAP OUR FAMILY AT THIS TIME, LEST I leave something important out. (Or someBODY!) Doug had his wife Kim and their two boys, Brooks and Gabe; and Mike and Beth had their three boys, Phil, Andy, and Lincoln. Phil, Beth's oldest, had Blake and Maddy so we were great grandparents and quite proud of that.

Doug was teaching at Liberty Center in the fifth grade, Kim was teaching at the Wauseon schools, and Mike and Beth both worked in Archbold, Ohio for Sauder's. Beth was in the corporate offices and Mike in quality control.

Phil ended up in a supervisory spot at Campbell's, and Andy is an on the road salesman and Lincoln, once he finished school, in the Army.

Linc had married prior to enlisting and he and Elisha were stationed in El Paso, Texas later as this time in our lives moved along.

If I completely chronicle these years from 1996 to present, you'll see God at work in every phase of life for us, but I want to stick to those times when we found God speaking directly to our lives, similar to our time in Pittsburg during Donna's brain surgery.

Donna slipped and fell down the final three or four steps into our basement and landed on her backside rather hard. She told me about it, but it seemed to have no effect on her for several years. However, along about 2012 she started having sciatic nerve problems and we figured it was a result of her fall.

There were times I would actually find her crawling through the house on all fours! I finally put my foot down and insisted she see a doctor. Well, I only partially won that battle because she went to see the chiropractor first. After several months of that, with little to no change, I finally won the battle and we went to a doctor in Maumee, Ohio.

She went through a series of shots that would help temporarily, until the pain doc recommended surgery and that was set up. Went through the x-rays, exams, and all that and finally she had the surgery. It consisted of a less than one inch incision and the enlarging of the exit place for that nerve from the spine and SHE WALKED OUT ON HER OWN THAT DAY! Life was good again.

All this time our church had our backs and kept us close to their hearts. That was good, because we would soon need more prayers than ever before from them and the family. Christmas night of 2012 Donna discovered a large lump in her left breast that was not there just a week or two before. I bundled her off to the doctor as soon as we could get her in.

Through the next few days' testing it was determined she had breast cancer. We wept together and determined we would fight this fight just like we had all the others, with God's Hand on our lives and faith in His love.

We were given the choice of a lumpectomy or breast removal and didn't even need to talk it over as the surgeon suggested. We both knew each other's choice just by making eye contact. Mastectomy.

The date was set and we cried our way home. I absolutely hated the idea that the love of my life had to go through yet another physical trial. She had survived so much by then, and had done it with a smile, unbelievable courage, and still praising her Lord Jesus. That was to remain her approach to such trials, for this one saw her no different in her approach. Prayer, praise, and peace.

This was to prove to be the mildest physical reaction to a major surgery she had experienced. The pain was low and short, her fatigue was the same, and we entered into a round of chemotherapy at the local hospital that would cause her much more discomfort than the surgery. We went once a week for nine weeks and she was sick as could be.

She lost her hair and was sick a lot, had diarrhea a lot, and was just miserable in general. She spent a lot of time in her recliner with big old Optimus Prime, our huge cat, on her lap. He seemed to understand her need for company and he would stretch his three feet of that big old twenty pound body from her tummy to her ankles for hours at a time. She loved it.

We were also doing radiation for six weeks at one point, driving from Napoleon to Maumee every day for a half hour at the cancer center there. The new four lane was, thankfully, open and it was a seventy mph speed limit all the way. I about wore the little Honda CRX out during that time.

With the chemo and radiation out of the way, the doctors declared her free of cancer but insisted on regular follow-up visits. We agreed. We had a wonderful summer that year and as her hair grew back it came in thicker and darker and my girl felt really good about that. Life returned to normal for us.

It's very hard to write anything detailed for this period because we were so wrapped up in each other that most of our time was spent just being together. No specific activities other than a lot of cuddling and smiling as we just took care of each other. We really didn't even talk as much as usual but simply wanted to be in the same room a lot of the time. The whole summer was sort of a remote blur together. It consisted of being home or church and little else. I even took a leave of absence from the elder board at church.

****

SOMETIME IN JANUARY OF 2015 DONNA HAD A follow-up doctor's visit scheduled and all was going well except she was having the leg pain again, this time in her left leg. The right had been cured by the back surgery two years previous and the sciatic nerve pain had been non-existent since then.

We met with the oncologist on a Monday and all went perfectly until he asked if there were any other problems. Donna said all was fine except she was having sciatic nerve pain again, but in the other leg. He got an almost panicked look and immediately ordered a bone scan. The cancer showed up, it was back, but this time in her spine at the base and some spots on her liver. It turns out that the spine is the most common place for breast cancer to metastasize and that was why he had the look he had.

Now it was back to the chemo once a week. We started that, and a few weeks into it, after her hair had begun to leave a again, he ordered another heart test. It showed her heart was working at 100 percent, so he recommended a more aggressive chemo be started that was proven 80% more effective than the others we had been taking.

The next day was Tuesday, her normal day for treatment, and so she started with the new chemo. Quite frankly, I think it killed her. No law suits, no bitterness, no spreading evil rumors about him as a doctor, but by that Friday she couldn't even get out of bed on her own, though she had been doing very well before.

Come time for her oncologist's appointment on Monday there was no way she could make it. I went in her place. As soon as I told him the situation he said it was time for them to call in hospice and that, if I wanted, they would make the call for me. I gave my permission because it seemed the time had come.

The next week was a blur, what with them calling in an adult potty chair and a wheel chair, putting the special kit of meds in the fridge, and bringing me a vial of lidocaine for topical use along with morphine for topical use. Those two were for the terrible sores in and on her mouth. Her lower lip was one big scab and the top was almost that bad. Her mouth was miserable. I applied those two meds often and they helped a tremendous amount.

Donna's tremendous will against pain became more and more evident as that week went on and my admiration never stopped growing. I talked almost non-stop to her during our waking hours, did a lot of rubs to help her comfort, and that became life for the time. Nothing else had a place in our being.

People's prayers were evident for us, and when Friday came so did the family. All of them. Doug and Kim and the boys spent all day Friday and well into the night; Beth and two of her three boys did the same, and the two great grandchildren were there most of the day. Beth's youngest, Lincoln, was in the Army in El Paso, Texas, and was to fly in on Saturday.

Having seen the effects of families trying desperately to hold on to a loved one who was dying and knowing it had been detrimental to the sick member because it kept them there way longer than it should have, which only increased the pain and suffering, I cautioned all of them to give Donna their permission to leave at any time she could. You may think me wrong or crazy, or both and even more; but I had seen it many times down through the years and it was something Donna and I had talked about several times even before either of us were sick.

Saturday: I woke in the morning to a wonderful lady just the same as when we went to sleep. Main difference was that she now could do absolutely nothing for herself, not even sit up. Any movement needed was up to me. I would pull her to a sitting position, get my arms under hers and literally lift her to the potty chair when she needed it. When done, I did the reverse and once in bed, I carefully helped her lie back down.

Pastor Kent came right after lunch that day and had a nice visit with her. She communicated mostly by hand signals but with as much of a smile as she could muster through the sores. I sensed the two of them had a really nice visit and later he would support that.

Sometime near the one o'clock hour I was rubbing her shoulders and arms and just rattling on about nothing when she looked up in my eyes, smiled as best as she could and spoke, "I don't think I'm going to be here long." It was a positive tone of voice with a definite spunky tone! I repeated my permission for her to leave.

Later on Beth was sitting on the bed and I was on the lid of the potty chair when she, all of a sudden, reached her arm and hand toward the other end of the room between Beth and me. It was an obvious welcoming gesture and Beth and I looked at each other. I said to her that "Mom is seeing angels!" Beth quickly nodded. That happened again many minutes later.

Around the two o'clock hour she was very restless and was tossing about. Beth was back out with the rest of the family and I was sitting beside her on the bed. I leaned down close and said in her ear for her to leave if she got the opportunity, and that Lincoln would understand. Her vocal reply was, "Oh, I have to hug him first."

Now, Lincoln had spent a tremendous amount of time with his Grandma during the summers playing monopoly in the pop-up camper and the two of them grew as close as any two people could be. Donna loved that young man with all she had.

Mike and Beth met him at the Detroit airport and delivered him to our house a little after six that afternoon. He walked into the bedroom, sat down by Donna and said, "Grandma, it's Lincoln."

She SAT UP under her own power, hugged him, and laid back down without just going plop, but a controlled reclining. They talked for quite a while and I knew my sweet lady wasn't going to be with us much longer; her goals were now all met.

By 7:00 she was asleep, never to wake again. She could be heard breathing deeply all night and well into the morning on Sunday. Unless I was in the bathroom or grabbing some food I was right there beside her in the bed, talking every waking moment. Her breathing through the day became more normal sounding, but with little hesitations between breaths, but still very relaxed with steady rhythm.

At 10:45 Sunday night as I lay with my arms around her she took a breath, then just a little catch, one more catch, and silence. My heart was torn from me as my life's hero slipped away to see Jesus face to face. One final miracle for this most awesome human being was complete.

I went out to the living room where the whole family waited and told them, "It's over." They all went in to say goodbye to Mom and Grandma while I called the hospice nurse.

We had both decided we wanted to be cremated when we died and when the hospice nurse asked who we wanted to come for the body I chose a well known funeral home in town. The young man came and he and the nurse cared for that task and we, the family, went our separate ways for the night. All but Lincoln, that is, for he would stay with Grandpa for those nights he would be here. I know it was a gesture designed to keep me company during these terrible first days, and I couldn't have appreciated it more.

We had the "visitation" time at the church, and then the memorial service right after. I made an error of judgment on that, for I allowed for two hours of visiting before the memorial service and there was still a really long line when the time for the service to start came.

I knew, of course, that Donna had touched many lives with her faith, but discovered that I really had not realized anywhere near just HOW many. The thing that touched me about that aspect of her relationship with Jesus was the huge number of people whom we did not have constant contact with who voiced emotionally how much her testimony had meant to them! Christ had shown through her so strongly. They say dynamite comes in small packages and my precious little stick of dynamite had blown many a hardened heart to pieces for Him.

****

THE FAMILY WAS WONDERFUL FOR ME AND DURING the first week after her departure helped me care for so many things associated with becoming a widower living alone. Beth was helping me clear her clothes from her closet during that week when she said to me, "Just think, Dad, Mom could be talking to Grandma and Grandpa right now."

My answer surprised her for I said, "I don't think so," and when she looked at me in surprise I said, "She hasn't taken her eyes off Jesus yet." THAT is how much I believe she loved/loves Him. I am totally serious.

Our lives together had involved thousands of miracles that stuck out beyond all else. God showed us Himself so many wonderful times, and if one of us failed to recognize His working, the other one made us aware of it. We were truly sent to each other, and for the purpose of bless-ing each other and caring for each other. Our marriage was fore-ordained by Him long before either of us knew of the other's existence. Don't bother trying to convince me otherwise; it won't get you anywhere because God has made it obvious many decades before the writing of this story of His love. (And ours.)

God blessed us so much as a family!

*Because of the Lord's great love
we are not consumed, for his
compassions never fail. They
are new every morning, great is
your faithfulness!*

Lamentations 3:22 (NIV)

Chapter Nineteen

I SHOULD TITLE THIS CHAPTER SOME-
thing like; "Living alone and lost" or something
like that. Our dear friend Amy and her kids, Matthew and Katie came over in the middle of the following
week to visit with me for a while as a comfort. That's the
way PMC people do, we serve and care for each other.

During that visit Amy shared a comment that had been
made to her at her mother's funeral. "Grief never stops,
it just changes." That comment from my very dear sister
has sustained me many times and I bless her and the kids
for that visit; it helped me at a time of deep sorrow.

There were other comforts expressed to me during
the next couple of months. People knew how close we
had been because there had been many comments on
our always holding hands or arms around shoulders, or
something like that and PMC had noticed those actions
of endearment.

You know how people always have those groups of
close friends in any congregation, even non-church clubs?
There are always those folks you make it a point to visit

with each Sunday and most others get a "Good morning" or a nod. I call those my casual brothers and sisters.

I cannot tell you how many of those "casual" acquaintances would stop me and hug me, pat my shoulder and go on without a word. Those many, many demonstrations of love went on for weeks. That is the way PMC Christians love, and their expressions of love meant a fortune to me.

I dare not leave Optimus Prime's actions out of this account. "Opti," better known as Kitty Baby, or just Kitty, was an orange and white cat weighing in at TWENTY POUNDS; he was THREE FEET long from his nose to the end of his tail, and stood FOURTEEN inches high at the hind quarters. I chronicled before how much of a lover he was to both of us, but now there is more to tell.

There were times he would sleep with us, but always down below Donna's feet and just barely on the corner of the foot of the bed. And usually not more than an hour or so. Early in the second week I awoke after a couple of hours or so in the bed with the sense that I was not alone. I opened my eyes to find a pair of yellow, glowing eyes about three inches from mine. It was funny because it seemed as though he was looking to see if I was really "in there." I touched him, petted him a couple of strokes and he laid down just inches from my face and went to sleep. He was there for hours and that became his practice from then on. He knew I needed him, or at least that is what I think.

He would wander through the house in the evening, sniffing Donna's chair from top to bottom, go off sniffing everything throughout the room, then come back, jump up into her chair, dig around for a bit, then plop down to sleep, but never for more than a few minutes. I was, and still am, convinced he was missing her. He was an absolutely huge comfort to me.

I am not a cook. Let me repeat that; I AM NOT a cook. A friend of mine commented on that same thing just this morning at church when he said, "I even burn water." As a result I was living on frozen food and meals that Beth baked for me and froze up that I could put in the oven so I wouldn't waste away to nothing.

I also became well acquainted with the menus and waitresses in town and even in Wauseon, Ohio, nine miles away. It got to the point where they knew what I was going to order today.

I continued building guitars and model airplanes in my shop, still competed during that summer, but not as much as before, and was just physically existing. My spiritual life was fine; this God would never let go of me and I didn't want Him to!

Donna died on the twelfth of July in 2015, and along about the last week of October I was down to just a little bit above miserably lonely. At home, that is. A men's group in Pettisville had invited me to a birthday party for one of their guys, and then invited me to join their group, which I did. Many of them belonged to PMC, though the group was not a part of the church, so they knew my story and I knew it was a kind gesture on their part to help me along. I still am part of that group called Pettisville Man Cave Ministries.

But...home life still stunk. For at least twenty years before any major illnesses had touched our lives we had always teased each other, though only half in jest, that, "If I go first, I want you to remarry or I'll come haunt you." We were serious about that.

When you have lived for fifty-one years with someone who was truly a part of you, alone is not a pleasant place to be. I had truly learned what the scripture, "And the two of them shall become one flesh," means. Many people think that refers to sexual intimacy, but I can tell you it goes so very far beyond that.

Many jokes and such have been made about married couples finishing each other's sentences and I'm sure that happens, but it wasn't a part of our relationship. But... looking each other in the eye and KNOWING what was being thought about a subject WAS. There was just a to-getherness that was constant, deep, and hard to put words to that existed between us; and others saw it and commented on it. We were, indeed, one.

Late in the third week of October I was praying as I worked in the shop and I said, and I quote, "Lord, my life sucks right now. If it is in Your plans for me to remarry, and please God, I hope it is, you are going to have to put someone directly in my face that I KNOW is Your desire, because if I go shopping I'll mess it up."

Less than a week later, Dorothy Smith called me. Dorothy had retired from Campbell's a few years before me and had worked in HR there, so I knew her from that, but after her retirement (Buy out) she had shared the duties of chairing the retirees' club. In that position she had learned of my first book being published and asked me to speak at their monthly luncheon. I gladly did so and we got to know each other as what I prefer to call "casual friends."

The second book came out, and she called again. So what prompted this call in October of 2015? Her oldest daughter and husband had been there visiting for a while and he had read all three of my books. He asked her if I had any more out and she decided to call me and ask. With just a little research she found my number and called. My answer was for her to email me her mailing address and as soon as the new book was in print I would send her a copy at no charge, just a little gift between old friends. After all, she HAD promoted my first two westerns.

When the email came and I saw her address was Oklahoma, I quickly replied with the question, what in the world was she doing THERE? Her reply sort of jarred me. Her first husband had died after forty-eight years of marriage and she had, after two years, met another guy who loved her, but he wanted to move to Oklahoma to be close to his oldest daughter. They did just that, but two years later, after nine years together his lung cancer came back and she lost him to that! She had been living alone for two years by the time this was taking place.

My next question to God was, "Is this from You?" We communicated via email for a bit, and in one of those emails she asked me if I had my tickets for the retirees' Christmas dinner. My reply was that I never bothered to go.

She said how she had missed doing the dinners since she had spent so many years co-chairing them and had actually priced airline tickets for 2015's event. But, between that cost and the cost for boarding her two little dogs she simply couldn't afford it.

By then I was wondering just what was going on between me and God, and I made the offer. I quote, "I can help you come back by paying for half the ticket and dog boarding if you really want to come. Plus, I'll furnish you a place to stay and transportation. The only hard-fast rule is, I TAKE THE COUCH! No arguments."

Donna and I had hosted many missionary couples at our house and they, each and every one, refused to take our comfortable bed. Our pull out couch was an invention of some medieval torture chamber designer. But, if only one person was going to use it still as a couch, it was very comfortable.

She agreed and the deal was made. What I did realize at the time was that she had told me she bought a house in Defiance, Ohio with the intention of moving back because two of her daughters who are still local had been almost insisting she come back to Buckeye land.

By now I was feeling rather convinced that God was at work, but figured her time back here for the week would prove or disprove the concept. I was totally prepared for either decision of His.

She spent nine days here, five of those with daughters, but we still saw each other every day. Each time we shared time together we drew closer and closer until I finally knew this was God's intervention. I shared that belief with her, we discussed our approaches to faith in Christ, and I ended up sending her back to Oklahoma with an engagement ring. I had fallen in love and so had she.

You can use the term "on the rebound" all you want, but when God sends you an answer like He did, you better listen to Him. That was a very quick answer to my prayer. One amusing thing I think about a lot was the contact we had at Campbell's. Dorothy had moved to the switchboard as her assignment and during the summer when Donna wasn't teaching I would get ready for lunch, take my tools off and grab the phone in my shop to call her and chat for a bit. I called it getting my daily dose of vitamin D.

I would punch "O" and when the operator answered I would say the same thing every day, "I need an outside line please." After about a week of that, the voice on the other end would say, "I'll dial her for you" without waiting for me to give her the number. Dorothy had come to recognize my voice and knew what I wanted. I just find that really fascinating to this day.

****

WE SET A MOVING BACK TO OHIO DATE AND I FLEW out to help her pack, load, and make the move. Her middle daughter Deb and husband Jim also went down to help with all that and I gotta tell you, without them, we would still be there trying figure everything out!

We married in April and settled down to housekeeping in my little two bedroom house with the two and a half car garage that resembled a warehouse! Her household stuff was stacked really high in there!

After a few weeks we started house hunting for a bigger house. We looked and looked, finding some that met the requirements we both had agreed on. There either had to be an out-building suitable for a shop for my guitar work, or room to build one.

The prices we were encountering were ridiculous and there was no way any of them was going to work Meanwhile, because of the combination of the move and long working hours then, as well as the radical life change I was undergoing, my atrial fibrillation reared its ugly head again and I had to see my cardiologist. He got me quickly straightened out with an increase in the meds I took for it and all was well again. But...after my follow-up visit we were pulling out of the Fulton County Hospital to head home when Dorothy repeated something she had said many times at that location. There was a beautiful tan brick ranch directly across from the hospital drive with a for sale by owner sign and a phone number.

I rejected the thought of calling about it because there was a white fence through the back yard and I thought the property ended there so there wasn't room to build a shop. Okay, okay, okay, we'll call! I gave in; we called, and looked at it the next day. It was a gorgeous place in near perfect shape, the back yard was twice as big as I thought, and when we heard the price we bought it on the spot!

The house had been on the market for two long years, and the price was ridiculously low! Dorothy and I thought it over and came to agree we think God had it waiting there for us all the time. Long story short, we built a 30' X 40' insulated shop that I keep at 62 degrees year round, and it is full of all my guitar building equipment and then some.

I have built more instruments back there in the two years since it was finished than in the previous five years, just because of the efficiency I can maintain.

Dorothy and I are very happy here together, I tell people I'm living the dream, and life in general is great. I shed tears nearly every day when little things happen that spur memories and make no apology for it. We talk freely about our previous spouses and I know she also hits the blurry eye syndrome often. Amy was right; grief never ends, it just changes.

****

I HAVE WRITTEN THIS STORY FOR ONE REASON AND one only; to glorify our great and wonderful God and to awaken people to the fact of His glorious presence EVERY MOMENT OF LIFE!

Okay, listen up, I'm getting on my high horse here and am about to preach at you. Every single one of us should look for and EXPECT miracles from God every day. The scripture teaches us that if we run to Him, He will run to us. He has demonstrated that to me ever since April of 1967. True, I haven't always liked His answer to certain prayers, but things always worked around to show me I was much better off with the answers He gave.

The best, safest, and most joyous place we can be is in His will for us. I had fifty-one years with Donna, just an incredible time, and I have now had nearly three years with the woman He had for me when He knew I was ready. I can testify that this is where I should be.

Why has God given me so many blessings? Why has He stayed so close to me and taken such wonderful care of me? Why me, and not the neighbor guy? The answer is this; He will take that kind of care of the neighbor guy if he serves God. He will take that kind of care of any and all who seek His presence and guidance. He LOVES me enough that He sent Jesus to die JUST FOR ME! Well, and just for every single human being who ever drew breath on this big rock we call earth. Yes, that means you, reader. All you have to do is believe that Jesus is the Son of God, accept that truth by confessing Him as Savior, and giving your life to Him. Read Romans chapter 10, verses 8 and 9. Then after you have given yourself to Him, read in the gospel of John, chapter 5, verse 24 and see what a fantastic future you have!

I want to speak to couples now; mine and Donna's lives together, and now mine and Dorothy's lives together are examples of what can happen when two hearts beat as one. My Christian life has been such a blessed one because of my helpmate. We never hesitated to challenge one another when it came to following him. I wrote earlier that the "two shall become one flesh" doesn't only refer to sexual intimacy in a married life, that two become one happens in the hearts and minds as well IF YOU LET IT!

Upon saying "I do" you must abolish self to each other. The old saying that a marriage must be 50-50 is messed up. NO! It must be 95-5! You must GIVE 95% of yourself to your partner with expectations of only receiving 5% in return. When your partner does the same, WOW! What a life you have together.

As I contemplate the skinny little hillbilly kid in southeast Ohio who dreamed of horses, airplanes, and guitars I am amazed at the opportunities he had to engage in every one of those activities, and not only participate, but do so at a reasonable success level. That, dear reader, is NOT brag on me, but a tribute to God's care over my life, even before I committed that life to Him.

It is also a tribute to a mother's prayers for her son. I remember Donna's amazement after a conversation with Mom during one visit. She had commented that Mom must have spent a terrific amount of time in prayer for me after I left home and Mom told her no. My mother explained her faith was that she had asked God for my safety in all parts of my life, she knew He heard her, and that was enough; God would take care of me, period. THAT, dear friend, is the kind of faith I wish I had in every part of life.

In closing, if each and every one of the people I love would read this, please realize YOU are a huge part of the blessings with which God has richly blessed me, and Donna, and Dorothy.

I have two of the greatest children any person could have, with equally great spouses; I have five strong and moral grandsons of whom I am most proud, and I have great grandchildren, multiplying rapidly, by the way, who will have to experience this morally deteriorating society without great grandpa spoiling them as they mature. My quiver is, indeed, full; as God referred to one of the great prophets in the scripture about his many offspring.

There is a quote I carry in my Bible that I absolutely love, it goes something like this: "The goal for the trip from the cradle to the grave should not be to arrive at the pearly gates with a well preserved and pretty body, but to slide in with a cloud of dust, used up, worn out, and loudly proclaiming, "Wow, what a ride!"

Can't remember who said that, but I plan to shake his hand right after my dust settles up there.

Shalom.

Dorothy and I as we venture into a
new chapter of our lives together.

About the Author

Will Riley Hinton was born and raised in the foothills of the Appalachians in southeast Ohio. He grew up on a farm with a grandfather who had made his living with horses and as a result, Will literally grew up on them. Having a mother who encouraged his active imagination along the lines of role playing and storytelling at a young age contributed greatly to his creative writing.

He was consumed by a love of horses, books, and airplanes. He served a hitch in the Navy and afterwards spent time as a part-time flight instructor and crop duster. Will has two grown children as well as five grandsons and five great grandchildren.

He is remarried and he and Dorothy now reside in Wauseon, Ohio, where they enjoy each other and their families.

Will builds custom guitars, sings in local venues such as senior centers and spends a lot of time at church activities, while Dorothy does a lot of time gardening and landscaping.

Other books by Will Hinton

The Rocky Mountain Odyssey series
Book 1: Lonely are the Hunted
Book 2: Rocky Mountain Odyssey
Book 3: Shadow of Vengeance

Also

Valley of the Shadow

Made in the USA
Columbia, SC
17 January 2023

75431232R00114